Soul Wisdom

My Journey through Self-Hypnosis

Janet Barako

Copyright © 2019 by Janet Barako
ISBN-13: 9781074620929

All rights reserved. Copyright under Berne Copyright Convention, and Pan-American Copyright Convention. No part of this book may be reproduced, stored in a retrieval system, or transmitted in any form, or by any means, electronic, mechanical, photocopying, recording or otherwise, without prior permission of the author.

Table of Contents

Introduction 1

Chapter 1: My Years with Rosie 9

Chapter 2: My Place 23

Chapter 3: "Of Course!" 29

Chapter 4: Reiki and Chakras 37

Chapter 5: The Visitor 55

Chapter 6: The Library 59

Chapter 7: The Books 65

Chapter 8: Spirit, Soul and Karma 85

Chapter 9: More Books 93

Chapter 10: The Gallery 115

Chapter 11: Memory Lane 125

Chapter 12: The Classroom 135

Chapter 13: The Secret Garden 145

Chapter 14: More Lessons 153

Chapter 15: Guides and Teachers 165

Chapter 16: The Turning Point 179

Epilogue 183

About the Author 187

Acknowledgments

I wish to thank all the people in my life that had the patience and understanding to support my efforts in the writing of this book, especially, my husband, Joseph. His loving support and encouragement made this all possible. I thank my daughters, Ann Marie and Michele for their understanding and support through the years.

To my sister, Marie, who carefully and skillfully helped to edit this book, a very special thank you. Many thanks go out to Cyd, Sandy, and Karen for allowing me to include their stories. I wish to thank the members of the Cape Cod Writers Studio for their help and support as well.

Last but not least, I have Spirit to thank for choosing me to be the vessel through which this book was written.

Introduction

"In a moment, I will count from one to three, and for each number I count, you will take a deep breath." With those words, I began my journey. The above sentence is frequently used in the beginning of a hypnotic induction, and, just to be clear, this book is not a "how to" book about hypnosis. However, I will show how it is a valuable tool I have used to reach into my deepest self, retrieving insight and a greater understanding of who I am than I could consciously ever do - retrieving my soul's wisdom.

Throughout this book I explain different aspects of hypnosis as I was taught. The word, "hypnos", is Greek meaning, sleep. However, when in the state of hypnosis, an individual is neither awake nor asleep. We can "zone out" and still be aware of our surroundings.

At this time, I should explain that all hypnosis is self-hypnosis. To begin the learning process, an individual may visit a hypnotherapist who will, by way of guided imagery, induce a state of relaxation. The hypnotherapist is not controlling but guiding the individual's mind. Eventually, with practice, the individual can recreate the process, and can self-hypnotize. The time it takes to be induced depends on the individual. I have practiced self-hypnosis since 1995 and the methodical induction process time has considerably shortened to only seconds.

My understanding is that hypnosis facilitates communication between the conscious and subconscious mind by way of induced relaxation. Therefore, hypnotic suggestions, such as, smoking cessation are more deeply embedded and accepted on the subconscious level enabling the individual to quit smoking.

I believe self-hypnosis helps us to control the chatter in our brains and allows our minds to focus our energy to where it is needed. Perhaps, mind over matter is then explained and healing of the mind and body can occur.

At first, when I began practicing self-hypnosis, my intention was primarily to simply relax. Through this process, I discovered capabilities I had no idea were possible. Though my method simply consists of relaxation techniques and self-guided imagery, it has been brought to my attention by others that my ability to reach such a deep level of trance is quite unusual.

This book is about my journey of self-exploration, of psychological and spiritual understanding. I am not trying to preach any kind of religious belief or convince you that there are other forces at work in our lives, though you can decide the latter for yourself. My hope is that you will keep an open mind and find my journals thought provoking.

As I allowed myself to explore the uncharted territory of my mind through self-hypnosis, I was so awed by the vividness of the experiences, I felt compelled to write about them after each session. For many years I severely questioned myself whether these sessions were real or "just my imagination". Each session was like reading a good book that I just couldn't put down, wondering what would come next in the story. There was an element of surprise in these sessions that was so astounding to me, that over time, I decided the experiences had to be real.

Before I proceed any further, I want to clarify my understanding of imagination versus reality. Imagination is part of the thought process, a creative function of the human mind. In the induction portion of hypnosis, imagination plays a large role as guided imagery, such as the suggestion of ocean waves to help relax the physical body. Most people are able to visualize or hear ocean waves as they have a memory or a reference whether it was a trip to the ocean or perhaps they have seen it on the television. Regardless, they are asked in the induction to use their imagination in order to achieve relaxation.

I believe imagination is a bridge to reality. I have often heard people say you have to experience something in order for it to be real, but imagination allows for vicarious experience.

Imagination is such an important part of being human. We depend upon it all the time. It is used in everyday problem solving and is the "mother of invention." Sadly, it is trivialized when someone says, "It's just your imagination." In other words, it is not real. It is not worth your attention. It can't be that important.

As a child, my parents would often say those words to me. They did not understand that I could sense and feel unseen energies. Those experiences were very real to me and I believed they were not my imagination. Certain areas of the old house we lived in seemed to be alive and positive while other parts of the house seemed verboten and negative. I could see moving shadows when nothing was there to cause them. I remember my childhood frustration as I could not explain this to anyone without being hushed.

After repeatedly being told what I saw or heard was not real, growing up I learned not to trust what I perceived as reality. If someone else could not validate my experience, I tried to not pay any attention to it. After all, it was "just my imagination." Consequently, I buried any extrasensory abilities I had as a child. I think it worried my parents that people would think I was crazy or different. I remember hearing my mother say, "The men in white coats will take you away." Actually, I think my mother had some abilities of her own which terrified her. Maybe, in her own way, she was only trying to protect me.

I believe imagination can also be thought of as an energy that resonates to a higher frequency referred to as Universal Consciousness, which I construe as an expansion of mind and spirit into a collective knowingness. For example, did you ever say, "For some reason, I just knew it was going to happen."? You did not have to think about it. You simply knew. Perhaps at that moment, you were connected to Universal Consciousness, the spiritual "all knowing" source which I believe holds knowledge of the past, present and future.

Over the years, I have concluded that the images appearing in my mind have been orchestrated by a spiritual guidance from the Universal Consciousness. This guidance helps me to understand whatever message I need to receive or to remember lessons from my past or present life that have been embedded in my soul. Mary, my spiritual guide, has always said, "You must remember." I simply have found a way to remember.

There is a place deep inside my mind that I refer to as My Place where I have received spiritual messages and insights as written in my journals and presented in this book. I find no other reasonable explanation for them other than being spiritually guided. It has taken me many years of soul searching to accept this as my reality as I tend to be very logical and analytical.

I believe through spiritual guidance, it is possible to search our souls and find the wisdom we already possess. Perhaps remembering lessons from our soul will help us achieve our greatest potential in this lifetime. I also believe we all are given a psychic blueprint when we are born that determines, in a similar way to DNA, who we are and what we may become. However, there are obstacles that come from living in this physical world that can impact our final outcome. We have learned behaviors, some good, some bad that will influence our lives, and, let us not forget, we all are born with the gift of free will to make choices. It certainly seems to be a daunting task to stay close to the plan, but I think if we pay attention to spiritual guidance, we can better reach our goals and potential. I believe our spiritual evolution continues to develop as we reincarnate into each subsequent lifetime.

When I decided to write this book and reread my journal entries, I realized there were some common threads, such as themes of fear, change, or choice representing some of the challenges I have faced in my life, leaving me feeling a little bit exposed. However, it is worth taking the risk of judgement if someone else can benefit from my experiences. I now feel I am better able to meet these challenges and enjoy living in this world and see my life with clarity.

As we look deep inside ourselves, many times the answers we seek are right in front of our noses, but they may be too close to focus and see clearly. Sometimes it takes someone else's thoughts and words to create a spark that ignites our own self-explorations and helps us on our journey in this life.

Symbolism is a key factor in the journals and has been, perhaps, the most difficult element for me to grasp, like a foreign language. However, over time, I came to think of it as a universal language. For example, the classic red rose can be seen to represent love as when given as a gift for Valentine's Day. Words are not needed to convey the thought or emotion.

As you will see, symbolism is utilized by Spirit in this way. Therefore, I see a deeper meaning in my experiences. Sometimes language has no words to express what Spirit wants to say.

I am certain that the communication I have with Spirit is called "channeling" which is explained in the next chapter. Perhaps the deep level of self-hypnosis which I experience has helped me connect with other soul energies as in the case of Rosie in the next chapter.

Throughout the book I speak of "soul" and "spirit". It has been extremely difficult for me to understand the difference between "soul" and "spirit" as both of these words are often used interchangeably, but I have attempted to explain them further to the best of my ability in Chapter 8.

I have experienced "artist's block" for many years having had extreme difficulty finding inspiration to paint again. Spirit helped me unlock the doors of my mind as you will see.

I was at a loss for a while deciding how to present these journals in a way that would be meaningful and easy to follow. The journals and other experiences have all been italicized and are dated in chronological order accordingly in each chapter.

I share in Chapter 4 other stories about healing energy by way of my Reiki practice. Even though Reiki has nothing to do with hypnosis, I felt it was necessary to include it as it has been an important part of my journey. The Reiki stories are powerful, and I feel are another example of our connection with mind, body and spiritual energy.

I am sharing my journals in the hopes that in them you may find insights into your own life experiences. As you read this book, please consider exploring the depths of your own thoughts as it may lead to the strengthening of your convictions, breaking down any self-imposed barriers and deepening the ability to trust in yourself. I believe, this process is important for self-evolution.

This journey of mine has led me down paths I never thought possible. Each question I had raised another and another. The quest to understand my experiences, as well as the encouragement of family and friends, overwhelmingly led me to write, and, in turn, the writing provided answers. So, now I invite you to sit down, get comfortable and join me on my journey.

Chapter 1

My Years with Rosie

I have begun the story of my journey with this chapter about past life regression as I feel it was the first step in opening my mind to the reality of another dimension of the human psyche and spiritual connection.

For most of my life, I believed that you only come once into this world. This belief probably stems from my Catholic upbringing where the idea of reincarnation is not encouraged. Certainly, we were taught that there is life after death in heaven, but not that we will come back again to earth as another individual.

In recent years, I have felt torn between religion and new ideas about past lives or what happens to us after we die. Many books have been written on this subject raising multiple questions in my mind and casting doubt on my early religious beliefs.

By way of hypnosis, past life regression, the process of retrieving memories from one's past either in this lifetime or a previous one, can be therapeutic. For example, if a person is unable to explain in this lifetime the reason for his phobia of flying, then regressing him to a time before he was born may produce an explanation. By asking him, during regression, to find a time when the phobia of flying began, he may be able to see himself as another individual living in a past life. Consequently, the individual re-experiences the event, under controlled conditions, which triggered the phobia. After some therapeutic suggestions, he returns to the present cured of the phobia.

     A skeptic might explain that the "memories" are simply a scenario created by the imagination. Perhaps rather than accept responsibility for our own actions or failings, this scenario allows us to see ourselves as another individual, therefore, passing blame for fears or behaviors to someone else. However, someone who has been hypnotically regressed would probably argue that during the session, he felt like another person. Afterwards he is then able to separate his emotions from the past life thereby releasing his present phobias.

     How I began my experiences with past life regression is quite simple. My husband, Joe, was the Director of Education in a local hospital that was going "Smoke-Free." He became a certified hypnotherapist to help the employees quit smoking. During his studies, he learned about past life regression which fascinated him. After he returned from his studies, I quickly became his first participant. To my surprise, I responded exceedingly well. I was an easy subject, often being regressed by Joe for similar demonstrations in the college course we taught about hypnosis which led to student certification. Each time he regressed me, the induction time would be less and less until I was able to reach a level of relaxation on my own.

A couple of years later, Joe was hosting a smoking cessation group with about six or seven individuals who were curious about past life regression. He suggested that I come to their session and allow him to regress me as a little demonstration for the group. I thought it would be fun. The deal was that I would sit in and watch them during hypnosis and then they could witness a past life regression through me. The purpose of the demonstration was to satisfy their curiosity and it was Joe's way of educating people about the "power" of hypnosis. This particular evening was the first time I met Rosie.

After a brief induction, I felt myself to be a young girl in the South who seemed very timid, nervous, and alone. In my mind, I stood on a cobblestone street and watched a cat run across the road in front of me. I then heard a man say something to me in what sounded like French. I looked to the right and saw a black, horse drawn carriage. The man helped me into the carriage. I sat on a hard, brown leather seat and the man sat in front holding the reins. The ride seemed rather long and very bumpy. I looked to the left and saw stores along the way. One store was a millenary with large fancy hats in the window next door to a bakery. The aromas from the bakery mingled with the odors of the horse and leather. It was warm that day, which intensified the odors.

Ahead there was a fork in the road. In the center was a large urn of cascading flowers. The carriage turned to the left. Soon after, the cobblestone turned to dirt. Then we stopped in front of a large, gray house. There appeared to be a brick sidewalk and a short, white picket fence. The house seemed surprisingly close to the road. The porch seemed wide enough for a comfortable rocking chair for one to sit on a nice cool evening, I imagined. The front door had a large, oval, designed frosted window.

A man greeted me at the door. He wore a black jacket with a white collar and cuffs, meticulously clean and starched. He escorted me to a small chair at the base of a large staircase where he told me to wait for "Ma'am" to come down to meet me. As I waited, I could see the sunlight shining off the highly polished wood floor. In front of me was a baby grand piano set inside a round alcove with long windows looking out onto a garden. I realized how small I felt. Inside I was trembling but refused to let it show through. The feeling of pride of where I came from, "up the river," seemed threatened by this new environment. I feared to lose the sense of who I was and uncertain of whom I was to become.

You must understand that when you experience a past life regression, it is much like tuning into a story on the television that has already started. You are not sure of the plot or characters, so you just sort of jump in and figure it out as it goes along. Up to this point in the regression, I didn't know who I might be.

As it turned out, I was to work for Ma'am as a housekeeper and the gentleman who met me at the door was George, the butler. I was given a tour of the house and gardens as part of my introduction. As I entered the Library, I was in total awe of the books and I gasped as I gazed at them. I had never seen a house like this before. Ma'am told me that in my free time I would be allowed to read any books that interested me and I thanked her. We then entered a small courtyard, which encompassed the entire back yard. It was paved in brick in a sort of wagon wheel design and had beautiful flowers. Hollyhocks grew up the side of the house and I could catch the aroma of all the flowers. I just knew this would be my favorite place.

Then, my husband, Joe, asked me to look at my arm and tell him what I saw. In my mind, I looked and saw a very young appearing, skinny, dark skinned arm. I thought, "So what?" Then he asked me, "What is your name?" I said, with confidence, "Rosie." I was able to give him much information, such as the year was 1893, the place was New Orleans, my age was 16, and I came from "up the river." He also asked me, "Can you read?" I told him, with some attitude, "Of course, I can read because my mamma taught me from the Bible."

Rosie may have been in awe of the books in the Library and insisted with pride that she could read, but, as I later learned, she was illiterate.

Joe then pushed me for more information and asked me, "Who is the President of the United States?" I quickly retorted with more attitude, "I don't care about some white man!" I refused to answer the question.

That was the end of our session that evening. The people in the group for smoking cessation seemed quite impressed with this unusual display. They specifically noted the change in my voice with a southern accent and my general demeanor, which was quite different from the person now standing before them.

Two days later, while watching the television and relaxing, intuitively, as though superimposed in front of my eyes, I saw the name, "Harrison" and thought, "President?" It took me by surprise and I said, "No way!" I ran downstairs and grabbed a history book. We didn't have the internet back then. Sure enough, President Harrison was in office in 1893. Remember, Rosie didn't want to talk about the President. Joe got his answer after all, and, to say the least, I got very excited.

Apparently, after experiencing hypnosis, people can retrieve information for a few days following a session. Hypnosis seems to unlock some pathways in the brain, even if only temporarily.

From that point on, Rosie seemed to take on a life of her own as she told her story. Whenever we did a demonstration of a past life regression for our students, Rosie would present herself as if she was aware there was an audience waiting for her. She was quick to speak her mind.

This became quite apparent when finally, one evening in front of the class, she started to converse with Joe. I have never heard of a past life character to speak unprompted. In fact, at times she seemed rather short tempered and confrontational with Joe. She then made known her desire to have her life story told as she deemed it, "Important." It was rather interesting how she managed to slip into my subconscious mind as if she had always been there. She may have been there a long time, as it seems.

Rosie's story continued to emerge one session at a time. Having had several regressions revealing different times and places in her life, I was finding it very odd that this particular character, Rosie, would be recurring as often as she did which is very unusual for past life regression sessions. I found that my ability to tap into her character became easier and quicker each time. Strangely enough, it seemed that she only came through when I mindfully invited her. I felt so comfortable with her presence that it almost seemed like I was visiting an old friend. I was beginning to feel an odd emotional attachment to Rosie.

As Rosie's story unfolded, I learned that she lived on the Mississippi with her parents, Adelaide, her mother, Benjamin, her father, and a little brother named Jeremiah. Her father's friend was the butler, George. He was the one who arranged for Rosie to work in New Orleans as a housekeeper for Ma'am. Any money she earned went back to her family to help support them. She did not have to worry about money because Ma'am provided everything for her. Here is the rest of her story.

At first, Rosie believed that Ma'am was wonderful because she was kind to her in the home. However, the first time Rosie was to go with Ma'am into the city, Ma'am's attitude changed completely much to Rosie's surprise and dismay. Rosie was told to walk behind her and not speak to her on her trip. She just could not understand what was wrong. She thought Ma'am liked her. She even saw her as a mother figure. She could not imagine what she could have done to deserve this. She held back the tears and did not say a word. When Ma'am entered a small store to pick up a package, Rosie followed her inside only to be told abruptly and sternly to wait outside as no "coloreds" were allowed.

Rosie had never been treated like this before and could not understand why all the fuss. Growing up, she had been sheltered from this behavior in her small community. I experienced her indignation, anger, and confusion. It broke my heart.

From that time on, Rosie felt lonely and was distrusting. Another session revealed the time when she first met her best friend, Mary, as she was walking to the stables one day. Mary was white and lived on her street. They were about the same age, probably late teens. It did not matter what was the color of their skin. It was as if they had known each other all their lives.

In one of the sessions my husband asked Rosie to find a happy time to remember. Instead of doing that, she started to bitterly complain about how hard she worked and that nobody cared. She was fussing and talking to herself when suddenly she heard someone calling her name. She explored the house and could find no one. She followed the voice to the back yard and suddenly she was greeted with a surprise birthday party. She turned 18 that warm day in June. There was food and cold lemonade. Her best friend, Mary, was there as well as George and Ma'am. Rosie had been feeling sorry for herself all day thinking that nobody remembered her birthday. No one cared. Her self-pity turned to pure joy and I felt it all. It truly was a happy time to remember.

When Rosie had some free time, she would frequent the stables to see a boy named Billy. She and Billy fell in love and wanted to marry. They were both young and strong but marriage meant that there was no place for the both of them to live in Ma'am's home. However, they would be very useful on Ma'am's horse farm. After they married, they were given jobs and a place to live. Apparently, Ma'am had a soft spot for Rosie. Life was good. They had two children, both boys.

Then hard times came along and Billy started drinking.

Once he was so drunk he chased Rosie out of the house and into the field with a big knife threatening to kill her. Fortunately, he passed out before he could hurt her. I could feel her terror.

During another session, Joe asked her what became of her sons. The oldest son was hung because he was accused of stealing a horse. Her youngest, about four or five years old, died of malaria. Rosie termed it "fever." Rosie also suffered from malaria as I had witnessed through one session. I experienced the suffering of the illness through her emotions. I did not feel physical symptoms. I could feel the weakness of her voice as the illness was draining her energy. It seemed that Rosie was progressively aging during the course of these sessions.

In one session I experienced her death. She said she was 80 years old. It was a warm and humid evening in what looked like the Bayou. She was resting in a chair on the porch with her old dog, Ruff, by her side. She wasn't feeling quite right and decided to go back into the house. She picked up her cane and entered a room that was painted yellow. There was an old-fashioned radio in the corner. She began calling for, Pa, her husband, when she collapsed on the floor. I could see through her eyes the wooden planks as she lay on the floor and felt the peacefulness as she passed. At that moment, I was back in the present finding it hard to express what I had just experienced.

After thinking about this experience, it occurred to me that Rosie could not be a past life of mine as she passed in 1957 when I was already seven years old. I was completely perplexed and could not understand how that could happen. As it was, Joe and I had planned a trip to New Jersey for a hypnosis conference. I have always enjoyed attending and listening to interesting presenters. One of the presenters was Dr. Irene Hickman, the author of, *Mind Probe-Hypnosis*. She was promoting her book about her work with patients and past life regression. We had the great opportunity to speak with her for a few moments, enough time to ask my burning question about how I could experience the death of a past life of mine if I was already born when Rosie died. I also explained the environment in the room when Rosie was coming and leaving, which I will explain later. Without a moment's hesitation, she asked me if I could have been near death at the time of Rosie's passing.

I realized that perhaps the timing might have been important in the fact that I did almost die at that age. When I was seven, I had, unfortunately, developed pneumonia on top of severe asthma. I was extremely ill. So ill that when our family doctor came to our house he feared taking me out into the cold to go to the hospital. Because I was allergic to Penicillin, he decided it was best to only give me intravenous fluids. In the early 50's there wasn't much in the way of antibiotics.

When I was ill, I vividly remember waking up one night feeling as if I were rising to the ceiling in my bedroom. I was terrified and tried to scream for my parents but nothing came out. I then remember floating into their room and seeing them sleeping soundly as I was trying to scream for their attention, but to no avail. Then in a flash, I was back in my own bed and able to scream.

Until speaking to Dr. Hickman, I thought maybe it was just a horrible dream. However, according to her, it was most likely an out-of-body experience or near-death experience.

The fact that I was clearly able to move about the house in that manner, said a lot to Dr. Hickman.

Dr. Hickman theorized that perhaps Rosie was not a past life of mine but rather that I was channeling this soul. This certainly made me take a step back and try to grasp this idea though it made perfect sense to Dr. Hickman. Channeling is explained as a soul entering a medium's body for the purpose of sending messages or in Rosie's case, telling her story.

Her matter-of-factness in turn made me a little frightened. She sensed that, and tried to further explain that perhaps Rosie was somehow attached to me. That thought did not make me feel comfortable. I then questioned, "How is this possible?" She could not answer but suggested that time would reveal the answer.

After our trip to New Jersey and having spoken with Dr. Hickman, we decided to try another session with Rosie. This time Rosie explained that at the time of her passing, she heard a child crying for his mother. She decided to follow the cry and not continue through the tunnel to the light. Since she had lost her young son to malaria, her love for him made her seek out the source of the cry in hopes of finding him. According to Rosie, the cries were mine and she claimed that her love energy brought me back. So, in essence, I guess I owe my life to her. She said she has always been there for me. Perhaps she has. It must have been difficult for Rosie to not find her son.

At the beginning of each session, Rosie had a strong energy. After Rosie made her point and told some of her story, her energy began to fade and I felt her getting tired and old. She then would say it was time for her to leave. When she stopped communicating and I was back in the moment, my body would react to all the energy and emotion by slight shaking. After a couple of minutes, when she had completely left me, I instantly stopped shaking and was back to my normal self.

There have been many times when a person sitting close to me has felt a cold breeze pass by them at the very moment I stopped shaking. There has been no explanation for the cold breeze especially being in a very warm room, which has been the case.

We did not prepare the students for anything they were about to witness before a session. All reactions by multiple people were similar in nature. Individuals who had been gifted with the ability to see an aura (light and color around people) would remark that when Rosie became evident in the classroom, my aura would expand several feet beyond normal.

Reaching this level of connection has allowed me to tell her story and experience her life through her eyes. I was able to feel the emotions as if I were in her shoes. I believe it was very purposeful that I sensed her emotions so deeply. It was as though they were being etched into my soul so as not to forget. Just think, here I am, a white woman in the 2000's able to express the feelings of a poor, young, black girl from the late 1800's. How bizarre is that?

I believe that only through the process of hypnosis could I have achieved this level of emotional/visual accuracy. The emotions then seemed to trigger the images in my mind. It is not quite like watching a movie. It is more like snippets, vivid snippets.

The last time I channeled her was shortly after Hurricane Katrina blasted through New Orleans.

I remember she appeared old when she arrived instead of her usual robust self, always exuding self-confidence. She seemed tired and sad. We assumed it had to do with the devastation of the storm. Joe asked about her old homestead and she said that it had already been destroyed years before. She was focused on the cemeteries and was very sad about that more than anything else. I could see in my mind's eye, very old monuments, with illegible inscriptions as though time meant to erase those memories. When she left the session, one of the students in front of the class stated that she could feel the ice-cold breeze pass by her.

By giving me glimpses of her life, Rosie has enabled me to see what it must have been like to live in the South in that era as a black woman. Through her eyes, I have seen and felt her hope, despair, love, happiness, anger, and final peace. These sessions have given me a unique perspective to furthering my understanding of human nature.

As of this writing, it has been a long time since I channeled Rosie. In the past, I have stated that if I were a writer, what wonderful stories could be told from my encounters with souls who have passed. Rosie deemed her story "important" and wanted it told. So, I hope I have fulfilled her wishes and in doing so, released her from her earthly bonds.

Chapter 2

My Place

The First Time in My Place
September 1, 1998

Today, I felt myself walking down a path in the woods. I remember looking down at my feet and noticed that they were bare. I felt crunching under my feet and smelled the dampness of soft green moss. I could hear the wind in the trees. I then noticed a few animals nearby. A small chipmunk darted across my path. There was a deer in the woods beyond grazing on a bush. I could hear an owl high up in the tree above me. Then I became somewhat surprised as I saw a wolf and a bear. However, I just knew that they would not harm me. They were there to greet me and protect me. I was not afraid.

Straight ahead was a door with five plain wooden steps. I opened the door and walked into a room. It took me by surprise, as it was no ordinary room.

I began to use all my senses. It was warm and

comfortable with a slight sweet scent of honeysuckle in the air. I heard the crackling of burning wood, which caught my attention so I turned to the right. I was facing a large fieldstone fireplace. It seemed to stretch across the entire side of the room. There was a fire burning in the massive firebox. I just knew it symbolized all the love in the world. It would never die out. I noticed the wood floor beneath my feet to be that of a beautiful parquet design. Straight ahead I viewed large French doors opening to a brick and gray granite patio. Beyond the patio was a perfect green lawn bordered by trees. An expanse of the ocean then spread past the trees down a steep rocky cliff echoing the sound of thunderous waves crashing below.

As I stood in the room, I noticed to my left the most striking feature that took my breath away. Books, all different colors, arose from floor to ceiling, dominating the entire wall. This Library was massive. I just knew that these books held all the knowledge of the Universe.

The ceiling was high with ornate, molded plaster designs painted in gold leaf. It all felt oddly familiar, yet, left me with a sense of overwhelming curiosity. Where was I, and how did I get here? I did not expect to see this sort of grandeur considering the plain woodsy appearance of the outside of the building. I thought the inside looked like a mansion.

Then, in my mind, I walked onto the patio only to find a small table with fancy petits fours set for two. I did not see anyone around but I remember thinking, "Now I have really gone over the top with this imagined place."

I decided it was time to come back to reality to my own living room. At that moment, I realized that my entire body was so relaxed, I felt as though I was part of the chair in which

I was sitting. It took a few seconds to feel my body and begin moving around again.

There is a part of hypnotic induction when the practitioner asks the subject to find, in their mind, the most beautiful place they could ever imagine. As many times as I practiced self-hypnosis, I found it difficult to decide which was the most beautiful place. I would flit from an ocean scene to a mountaintop, to a meadow, or wherever I could think to go. I just couldn't settle on any place.

I never experienced anything quite like My Place before and with such surprising clarity. Sometimes the clarity of the details I see in my mind are amazingly sharp, while other parts of the scene are just impressions or blurry. It is as if my eyes are the lens of a camera adjusting to a narrow focal point.

Had I gone to a deeper level of hypnosis? My Place did not seem preconceived as I truly felt in awe of its magnificence. I thought about the books and wondered what stories they told. What I had experienced was definitely addictive and I wanted to return to that state of mind or place. It captured my curiosity and it was quite pleasant and very real to me. I was comfortable and felt safe. Clarity came with focus.

Mary told me all the information stored in the books are the imprints of the memories and thoughts from my many life experiences over millennia. With so many lives, how could I not gain some wisdom? Since energy is timeless, even the future may be written.

I feel it is important to note that before I proceeded with any session, I have always asked God, the Highest Power of Good, for protection and enlightenment.

The Second Visit
September 16, 1998

Again, I traveled through the woods and entered the mansion. To my surprise, I found someone sitting at the table on the patio. It was a woman dressed in a blue and white, rough woven, hooded robe. I could not see her features clearly at all, because there seemed to be a great deal of light emanating from her face, yet, I was aware of a smile. I noticed her delicate hands gracefully placed on the table. I suppose my Catholic background contributed to my assumption that this person must be Mother Mary. Again, I was quite surprised by her presence, immediately questioning why she would be there with me.

She led me to the Library inside the mansion. I asked her what this place was and she said it was my "home." I remember thinking, "Yeah, right!" I had no idea that my imagination was this good!

So, I thought, if this is my imagination, then there certainly is nothing to worry about. After all, I am safe in my own living room. I ended the session with that thought.

Despite my attempts to try to understand what I had been experiencing, I decided to just go with it and enjoy exploring this new pastime of self-hypnosis. My sessions took only about 15-20 minutes. From the beginning I began to write down in a notebook some of my experiences so as not to forget. Not all sessions were notable, but some were very insightful. Many times, I went to My Place with a question on my mind about something that was bothering me or because

I was just curious.

Often, I was baffled by what I saw and felt in the mansion and I had to constantly ask Mary to explain things to me. Most of the time she did. Other times, she left it up to me to figure out the puzzle. All the books that I had been shown were quite unique, as you will see.

An abundant amount of symbolism is in My Place. Everywhere I look there is hidden meaning from the books to the fireplace and so on. If you think about it, our homes are symbolic of who we are. In other words, our creative energy forms our environment. Our homes say a lot about us, such as, whether we are well organized, what are our favorite colors, style of furnishings, etc.

After I became familiar with the Library, I was shown other rooms in this magnificent place when Mary thought I was ready. I even had a "Secret Garden." Occasionally I visited "Memory Lane." Apparently, I reference clichéd names of places.

I frequented a room called the "Classroom." This was probably my favorite room. It was a different kind of classroom without books or chalkboard. The seats faced a huge window with views of rolling hills and fields. Mary told me that Mother Nature is my teacher. This reference will also be explained later.

Mary once told me, "Simplicity leads to completeness." It really is true. I believe that we tend to make things more complicated than necessary, leading to confusion and overwhelming us. Taking one step at a time allows us to focus more clearly and completely on the task at hand. Then when moving on to the next task, anxiety is greatly reduced. It has taken me years to see this process at work. Each time I went to My Place, I was able to focus better. Sometimes I had to remind myself to focus, such as, when I was given a book from the Library to view or given a specific situation.

Mary has said, "Serenity is a path, not the result." Often, I have heard people say they just wanted to feel peace and serenity. Maybe they have lost their way. If they were on the path of serenity, there would be less anxiety. They would know where they were going. There would be a focus in their life. For instance, anger would be replaced with peace and fear would be replaced with trust - all idealistic, but true. Certainly, complicating things does not feel serene. I can only guess what she meant by "result."

There are so many aspects of my life that could take a lifetime of introspection to understand. Just as I thought I might have an indication of who I really was, and, perhaps even my purpose in life, more questions were opened for exploration. It seems this could be never-ending, a constant need to get more answers only to be met with more questions as you will see in the next chapter. The fun is in the process.

Chapter 3

"Of Course!"

Cyd is a dear friend whom I respect and admire. We met when she enrolled in our hypnosis class through a local community college. I remember the first time I saw her. She was well dressed compared to the other students in the classroom that wore more casual attire. I only could assume that she had rushed to class from her work. I remember saying to Joe, "That lady looks like an intellectual." Her hair was very curly and she wore large glasses that seemed too big for her face. Cyd had a pleasant smile but a reserved demeanor. She did not say much in class but took many notes. Very few people took notes. Since there was little verbal interaction during the course, it was fair to say that we did not develop a relationship other than teacher to student.

Cyd, a psychotherapist, took our hypnosis course to explore other methods of therapies to help her clients. I thought she seemed very nice and someone I would like to get to know. However, the class ended and I did not see her again until the day I agreed to share the rent of half of an office space with a Reiki practitioner in West Springfield. (Reiki will be explained in the next chapter.)

At the time, I was a massage therapist and wanted to move my practice out of my home. Unbeknownst to me, Cyd had already been renting the other half of the office space and we were quite surprised to find each other again.

Was this a coincidence? I really don't believe in coincidence. There is a reason for everything even if it makes no sense at the time. Hindsight is 20/20. Some people ignore what they consider to be a coincidence. They prefer to think of it as mere randomness. Others take note of the coincidences and search for some kind of connection or meaning. For me, I believe coincidence is another way the Universe has to manipulate humans. In other words, when we are not making the right connections, the Universe figures another way to help us do so. Well, at least, I like to think this way. Regardless, Cyd and I finally got to know each other and discovered we had a great deal in common. As it turns out, Cyd is a very spiritually minded person and open to learning as much as she can about the human psyche and our spiritual nature.

Over the next several months, we had stimulating conversations. I began describing my experiences to her. At the time, I was unsure what people might think if I explained where I take my mind in the hypnotic state. I had a fear of being labeled as a little flaky or, heaven forbid, "crazy." However, much to my relief, Cyd reassured me that the latter was not the case. She had a way of putting someone at ease.

She became quite interested in my experiences so we decided to try something new. I was to go to My Place and Cyd would record my session. Not only did she record everything I said, she also wrote down everything I did including pauses and gestures. Those sessions were a challenge for me as it took a great deal of effort to speak due to the deep level of relaxation that I would reach. Plus, when I am at that level, my thoughts are so rapid that my speech cannot keep up. I have included these sessions, unedited, as Cyd transcribed them so as to demonstrate my demeanor as observed by Cyd.

Cyd has always been my first phone call after I would journal about a session. I would be very excited to share my newfound insight only to be greeted with, "Of course!" To my utter amazement, Cyd would say, "Hold on while I get a book." Cyd had the tendency to buy books that "spoke" to her. Low and behold, sure enough, she would have recently read something relative to my hypnosis experience.

It drove me crazy! How on earth did that happen over and over again? In a way, it sort of burst my bubble of excitement that I discovered some new insight from My Place. At the same time, there was a validation, which would provide a feeling of assurance that I was on the right path. Cyd explained to me years later that my sessions would help her understand what *she* had just read. That is why she said, "Of course!"

There have been a few times that Cyd asked me if I could visit Mary for her. I had no idea if this was even possible until one relaxing weekend we spent at Cape Cod in Massachusetts. Cyd wondered if I would be able to reach Mary that evening to see if she could receive any messages. I said that I would certainly try. Cyd did not have a recording device so she wrote in long hand the best she could. Here is the unedited transcript.

Cyd's Truth
September 9, 2000, 8:10 PM

Jan regressing to the room. Done at Cape cottage. Purpose-to ask Mary if there is a book that will help me in the search for truth.

In woods. A strange sensation came over Jan like spinning to the right, not nystagmus. Jan came back.

"Entering the room. Hmm, It's nighttime there. I've never been there at nighttime. There's a light on. I've never seen lights before. I don't see Mary there. It looks like a note on the table. I think the note is directing me to something. I think it's a book. I don't know. Hmm, there is a blue book and it's kind of shoved out from the others. OK, I've got it. It's like a children's book. This makes no sense. It's 'Brer Rabbit'. I don't get this. Why is this significant?

"Oh Good! She's here finally. She says to look deep into the words. That's where to find the answer. I asked her if she could help you (Cyd). She said you'd find the way. I asked her if you are going to find the truth. She said the truth is behind the wall. The wall of the mind. You (Cyd) built that wall. I'm going to ask her if these are all the truths. She says it's the truth in human terms. If you reach into your heart, you see the truth. Clarity is a virtue. Honesty is an attribute. Combine the two and you will find the answer. Solitude is a must. Praying is an absolute."

"She said I took a great chance to come there tonight. At nighttime I should not walk in the woods, I asked her if it was okay I came and she said I had a mission. She said she would always protect me. She said there are great mysteries

to be unfolded and you (Cyd) will do it. It's time for me to go."
Finished 8:22 PM.

We never tried to figure out what the story of Brer Rabbit was supposed to mean. I remember reading the story as a child, but looking deep into the words for a hidden meaning, just did not seem intriguing enough to pursue. Perhaps it was really meant for Cyd, not me. I don't know. I guess time will tell. Sometimes, the purpose of a message is not understood until much later, even years later.

As far as the message that Cyd received, I can only surmise what Mary was trying to tell her that she placed her own barrier, the wall, in her mind. Maybe she subconsciously was protecting herself from the "truth." Only Cyd knows for sure.

Mary stated that clarity is a virtue and honesty is an attribute. In other words, to find the truth, you have to communicate clearly with your own soul and be honest with yourself. Otherwise, you are only fooling yourself.

Mary also mentioned solitude and prayer. You need to find a place to disconnect from the world and avoid distractions for a while in order to see more clearly. If you find difficulty, pray for answers. The Highest Power of Good is always listening. Mary always said, "You have to ask." Make your intentions clear and never be afraid to ask for help. I believe we will be answered in some way. It will be for our highest good.

Later that evening, as I sat on my porch looking at the stars over the ocean, I felt a sense of joy that this "gift" had now helped someone else. I realized that I could share the insights that come about from the visits to My Place.

Several years later, Cyd was again seeking some words of comfort from Mary. However, this time, the information had a new direction. Cyd had undergone a great deal in her life. This time, I journaled the session. The following is the entry I wrote that day.

**Cyd and the Bible
January 3, 2007**

It has been too long since my last entry. There is much to catch up. Cyd came home very ill from Micronesia where she went for a short time with the Peace Corps, but she is getting better. My friend, Beverly, passed on Christmas Eve day. I feel drained much of the time. I need to regenerate.

I find it extremely easy to visit Mary so much that I forget or just have not taken the time to write about it. I find myself more in the Classroom (explained in Chapter 12) *than anywhere else lately. Before Beverly passed, I asked Mary what I could do for her. I guessed just praying. Mary said to tell her a secret. She said, "Listen for the white spirit whispers." I never got the chance to tell Beverly but I think she knew.*

My friend, Cyd, asked if I could go to Mary and ask her if she could help her as she was searching for some comfort. So, I did with Cyd present.

I was in the Classroom and saw that it was raining outside. Mary then handed me a Bible. It was the first time I ever saw a book in the Classroom. I opened it and placed the ribbon marker on a page that was about three-quarters of the way through the book. In the lower left-hand page, I saw some letters instead of numbers. I asked Cyd to hand me a pen and paper. With my eyes closed I copied what I saw. It looked like a fancy L and II with some red ink near it which was unclear. Then I thanked Mary and opened my eyes.

When I showed Cyd what I wrote, she immediately said it was the Roman numeral 52. After Cyd went home, she looked through a few of her family Bibles. Finally, her mother's Bible had the answer. Just as Mary showed me, Cyd found the verse about three-quarters of the way into the Bible on the left-hand side, numbered 52. Cyd said it gave her the comfort she needed. Amazing!

Even as I was experiencing this session, I realized that the message had to be for Cyd because none of it made sense to me. I have never even owned a Bible. Growing up, my family did not have one either. My only recollection of a Bible was what I saw in the pews at church on Sundays in my younger years.

It was difficult to relay just what Mary was saying to me, as she spoke rapidly. I was afraid I would miss something if I took the time to repeat everything to Cyd. I could not take the time to explain all the sensations and details of what I was experiencing. My focus was so clear I could feel the silkiness of the ribbon marker as I slipped it between the pages of the Bible. I could feel the soft leather of the book's cover.

I remember how excited and relieved Cyd's voice sounded on the phone when she called me to tell me she found the verse. She said it really was what she needed to read. Cyd was pleased to receive her message. This experience reinforced the reason I wanted to write this book. Certainly, Cyd was also encouraging me to write.

This session with Cyd and the one before left me with a positive feeling just knowing that my friend benefited from the experience. It also left me with an eerie feeling. It seemed that Mary knew I was coming to My Place ahead of time and was waiting for me with the answers in hand. If you asked me before the last session if I knew how to write the Roman numeral 52, I would have laughed and said, "Are you kidding? Of course not." I probably learned Roman numerals as a kid but forgot them. Cyd, on the other hand, was well aware of Roman numerals due to her extensive background.

During the session, I did not feel any connection with the Bible or the verses. It was definitely geared toward Cyd and her needs at the moment. At the time, I asked myself if this could be a validation of the existence of Mary as a true entity and not my imagination. It certainly made me stop and think how I could have received this information. It did not seem to have come from some inner wisdom of my own. I questioned if this was what occurred every time I journeyed to My Place. I wondered if these insights and information were generated from some other source. I began to think that if this is another source, that it must be helping me to reach for the wisdom deep inside. I felt uncertain. Once again, I was left with more questions. Of course!

Chapter 4

Reiki and Chakras

REIKI

Throughout this book, I reference Reiki and Chakras. Hopefully, this chapter will help to explain a little about both. As stated in the introduction, Reiki has nothing to do with hypnosis but, it has been an important part of my journey. Reiki is a completely different healing modality. I have been a Reiki Master for over 20 years. During this time, I have learned far more than I could have possibly imagined about healing from the emotional aspects to the physical.

There are many books written to explain in great detail what Reiki is all about. It is my goal to simplify the explanation and tell my story. Reiki is a unique energy healing system. There is no way to know exactly when it began. It is thought that our ancient ancestors about 2,500 to 3000 years ago were able to tap into the energy of Universal Life Force to heal themselves and animals. I will explain more later.

How did I get into Reiki? Here is my story. Most of my adult life I earned a living with medical transcription. For 30 years I had my own home-based business. However, the many years of hunching over a typewriter took its toll on my neck and back. I sought relief from a chiropractor for the first time. Unfortunately, I was so limited in movement, that the chiropractor had extreme difficulty releasing my neck and back. He suggested I see the acupressurist first. All of this complementary medicine was very foreign to me as I was only familiar with allopathic western medicine. However, I was willing to do anything at that point.

After a couple of visits with the acupressurist, I began to loosen 30 years' worth of stiffness and pain. I was very impressed with this process and began to inquire about the education involved in this new mode of treatment. I liked the one-on-one setting. It certainly beat the solitude of my business and the cold interaction with a bodiless voice from my transcription machine.

I came to the harsh realization that I have been in the wrong business! After some soul searching, I decided to make a mid-life career change. I enrolled in a well-known accredited massage school. I had just graduated from college with my degree in fine art and now I was telling my family that I was going back to school for two more intensive years. Fortunately, I have an amazing husband and kids who were completely supportive. Massage school was hard work and I loved every minute of my training. It was during that time that I was incidentally introduced to Reiki.

At first, I thought Reiki was some strange practice that I would prefer to avoid. However, one day I went to massage school with a pulled muscle in my back. I could hardly walk.

This condition would happen to me periodically and I would be out of commission for a week or two.

Two fellow classmates said they were Reiki Masters and offered to do some healing for me on our break time. I was in such pain that I agreed to whatever could help. They simply lightly placed their hands on my back. The only thing I could feel was a little warmth but no pain relief. I thanked them for their efforts. About an hour later, I noticed some mild relief. The next morning, my back was perfectly normal. I still was not sure if the relief was related to the Reiki, but my curiosity was piqued.

My introduction to Reiki coincided with the hypnosis course my husband and I were teaching in the evening at a local community college. During one of the student's self-introduction, he stated that he was a Reiki Master. Guided by my newfound interest, I approached him after class and he agreed to attune me to the first level of Reiki. With some trepidation, I went ahead with the attunement. It just so happened the evening of the attunement, I was suffering from a severe headache. I thought, surely, the headache would be gone after the attunement. Nothing happened! I still had a headache afterward and I thought it was a total waste of time and money. I was truly disappointed.

Two weeks later, Joe came home from work and told me that one of his coworkers at the hospital came to work with an Ace bandage wrapped around her foot and she was wearing a slipper. Apparently, she had a severely inflamed bone spur in her heel. He said he told her to stop by our house on the way home from work and suggested that maybe I could help her. I told him that I could not do anything for a bone spur with massage. He then mentioned I could try the Reiki. I quickly retorted that I did not think it would work.

Sure enough, she stopped by on her way home. This was the first time I met the lady. I explained that I really did not think I could help her, but Joe had insisted that I try the Reiki. She was in so much pain she would try anything. I reluctantly agreed to try the Reiki.

Much to my surprise, I noted some strange sensation in my hand as I held her heel. Then, for some unknown reason, I stated, "The pain might increase, but I will stay with it until it goes away." As soon as I said that, all I could think of was, "Why did I just say that? What if it does not get worse, or what if it does and it does not go away?" It did get a little worse and then got a little better but she still left with the original pain. I felt ridiculous and embarrassed.

The next day she stopped by our house on the way home and she presented a beautiful plant as a thank you. I felt very embarrassed as I said, "You did not need to do this as I did not do anything." She said, "Oh really? What do you call this?" I looked at her foot and she was wearing her normal shoe and claimed to have no pain whatsoever. I was stunned. She said she even canceled her appointment for the cortisone shot even though I advised against canceling.

That was over 20 years ago. The pain in her heel never returned. This incident catapulted my use of Reiki into my everyday life. Since then, the healing stories abound, far too many for this book. However, I would like to share a few that are dear to my heart.

My mother was extremely skeptical about my newfound passion. I am not sure if she was afraid of the Reiki or if she thought it was hogwash. However, once in a while she would allow me to practice with her though she claimed it had no effect on her.

Mom was in her 80's when she began to get unsteady walking. One day she lost her balance and fell into the outstretched recliner into the empty space between the footrest and the chair. She apparently tore the muscles of the rotator cuff in her shoulder. The result was extreme pain radiating to her neck. Because her injury was so severe and her age factor, surgery was out of the question. She sought help from a local pain clinic informing her that nothing could be done to alleviate the pain. Mom was devastated.

That afternoon I tried to comfort her. I suggested a little Reiki could help to relax her. At that point, she was more than willing to do anything if it could make her feel any better. I proceeded to perform a head to toe Reiki session. As I was finishing, my intuition told me to go back to her shoulder and concentrate on the injury. I held one hand behind her shoulder and the other held lightly on top. Suddenly her shoulder shrugged. She opened her eyes and asked, "What did you just do?" I said, "Nothing." Then I felt her shoulder press hard into my hand, followed by a rolling sensation. I looked at her with amazement as she said, "The pain is gone." We felt guarded excitement and relief. Whatever had occurred was so miraculous that it seemed to be divine intervention. The following week my mother had a routine doctor appointment. I would always go with her into the exam room as her hearing was very poor and could not always catch what was being said.

The physician asked Mom about her shoulder. She replied, "Well, my daughter is a little *strange*. She did Reiki on my shoulder and the pain went away." I wanted to disappear into the wall at that moment. Really? "Strange"? Thank goodness, the physician knew what Reiki was and had a good sense of humor as she saw me sink down into the chair and hide behind my hand.

From that point on, Mom never questioned Reiki again. In fact, I would use it quite often as panic attacks began to cause trips to the hospital Emergency Department. The panic attacks were horrible as she felt she was about to die, so she would call 911. Upon arrival to the hospital, I would immediately begin Reiki to help relax her and the symptoms would subside. After all the workup was completed and everything was normal, she would be released.

At the end of her life, she suffered a cerebrovascular accident in the brain. She had difficulty swallowing and developed aspiration pneumonia. Hours before she passed, I stood by her bed and did a little Reiki for her.

Reiki is also used to help with the transition into death. Mom was not aware of my presence as she labored to breathe. I simply held my hands a few inches away from her body and with a sweeping motion drew them from her head to her abdomen and up in the air. As I did, her whole chest and abdomen rose up off the bed slightly as though I were pulling her up like a marionette puppet. Joe and I looked at each other in utter amazement. Joe said, "Do it again." I repeated the motion and again, her body followed my hands. I felt as though I was pulling her out of her body but she was not quite ready to leave. Hours later she passed.

For twelve years, I worked at a local cancer center every Friday providing Reiki sessions to cancer patients or their caregivers. I looked forward to working with these individuals not only for their amazing healing but what I could learn from their experiences.

The main objective of Reiki for the cancer patients was to help with relaxation. Having cancer is certainly stressful and the treatments are usually accompanied with uncomfortable side effects. Relaxation techniques are valuable in coping with pain and nausea. Most of the time patients are relieved from the symptoms. Many times, they also receive unexpected healing. One possible reaction to Reiki is slight involuntary muscle twitching which is not uncommon. However, what happened to one patient was so unusual that I was compelled to videotape two of his sessions.

The gentleman was a 75-year-old diabetic who had multiple sclerosis (MS) and inoperable bladder cancer. He was rather obese and walked with a cane. During the first session, he started to laugh when I was working on his feet. I remember him saying, "The Leprechauns are tickling my feet." At first, I thought what a funny thing to say. He then told me that was the first sensation he had had in his feet since the diabetic neuropathy left him with complete numbness.

Six months later, in the beginning of a session, I noted that his big toe began to twitch followed by the entire foot, then both feet, then before I knew it, his legs were kicking up and down. He was hanging onto the Reiki table and laughing saying, "I can't stop it." I could not believe what I was seeing. My immediate thought was he was having a seizure. However, he was clearly conscious and able to communicate so I quickly determined it was not a seizure and perhaps it was related to the energy work. Thank goodness, it was the Reiki. From then on, each session he exhibited the same reaction. Within five minutes of the session, it would begin and continue for 15 to 20 minutes at a time. He had no ill after effects and would feel better until the next session. He mentioned that after each session, he stopped dropping things, which had been a common symptom of the MS. I saw this man for three years until I had surgery for my ruptured disc. He stopped coming to the cancer center during the period of my recuperation and passed away only five months later. We used to joke about making him famous because of his extreme reaction to the Reiki. I hope his soul is pleased that I have told his story.

Before every Reiki session, I ask for protection from the Highest Power of Good. I want to be sure that only positive energy is allowed into the session. Quite often at the end of a Reiki session, but not every time, I will have a spirit that wishes to communicate some message to my client. This is how it happens.

My first inclination that a spirit is present is to feel cold on my right side. Then I tune in and ask the client's permission to proceed. When I get the go ahead, I then begin to feel a sense of peacefulness on my back. I close my eyes and, in my mind, I ask the soul to show me something that the client will know who is with us. As I open my eyes, in my mind's eye, whatever I see, I announce to my client. (It is something like day dreaming. What I see is sort of superimposed in front of my normal field of vision.) As a rule, the client will understand right away what it means to them. Most of the time I will also hear a name or see it if I ask the spirit. The ways of communicating vary with each spirit. Sometimes I am given a virtual tour of a physical place with which the client is familiar and there is no auditory communication. Other times, it is only auditory or visual. The following story is a good example of both.

Many years ago, I was conducting a Reiki session with my good friend, Karen. This was the first time Karen's deceased brother made himself known to me.

Her brother was describing a scene which Karen was able to validate as having happened when, suddenly, I heard her brother say to me, "Your sister is going to be alright, you know." I was stunned, as I had recently received the news of my sister's probable condition being a stage IV cancer. I immediately told Karen what I had just heard from her brother when she exclaimed, "I just asked my brother to give YOU something!" It was a moment I will not forget. Months later, I was informed that my sister was cancer free and she still is alright after 10 years.

This Reiki session was a surprise to me and to Karen. My hope is that this example shows the power of our spirit. Just spirit presence can be emotionally healing. I believe that if you pay attention to the unexplainable, perhaps Spirit is the reason for those happenings. Someone might be trying to tell you something.

Of course, the fear of the unseen and intangible is understandable especially when you are alone. Who sleeps well after watching a horror movie? I am sure negativity does exist. If I should feel uncomfortable sensing anything negative, and I have, I try to remember that negativity feeds off fear and then my thoughts instead turn to pity. Pity that the spirit entity is unable to feel love or be in the light. Following such an encounter, I instantly felt it withdraw and leave me alone.

In all the years I have been doing healing work, I have never dealt with any negative spirit in any Reiki session with clients. As I always ask for protection, I feel that the positive energy during these healing sessions allows only goodness to enter and always feels calm and serene as if it were the most natural thing in the world.

After the sessions are over and I have time to reflect, I often find myself amazed at what transpired. I never take it for granted and always feel honored that a spirit would choose me to be the conduit for their message.

It is believed that Reiki heals the ethereal, or aura (I use aura and ethereal interchangeably) as well as the physical body. Our ethereal body extends beyond our physical body by a few feet. There are people who are able to see these auras and have reported visualizing colors as well. There have only been a couple of times that I could detect a color surrounding an individual. I thought at first there must be something wrong with my eyes. I looked away to someone else and saw nothing unusual only to return my gaze to the first person and again saw the color green emanating from his body. It struck me as very odd yet fascinating.

I also believe that the aura, being our soul energy, holds memory from both past and present lives. Upon our passing, this memory is carried on with our soul energy. I have discussed this idea of the soul and spirit holding memory in Chapter 8.

Theoretically, if the memory is negative or traumatic, perhaps a lowered frequency and vibration level could cause a weakness to develop in the aura making the physical body susceptible to disease. I believe that our auras are a defense mechanism, which needs to be kept healthy just as much as our physical body's immune system.

During Reiki sessions, I often have experiences of tapping into a client's memory, describing events from their past in great detail which can be healing. The following story is an example of such an event.

It was the end of a Reiki session when I suddenly felt a cold chill on my right leg which is usually indicative of a spirit entity trying to get a message to the person who is with me at the time. I cautiously asked my client permission to pursue the message. Without hesitation, she said, "Yes, by all means".

I proceeded to close my eyes and began to feel a peaceful sensation on my back. In my mind, I asked the entity to show me something that my client would understand. As I opened my eyes, I could see a pile of potatoes. I remember thinking, "How strange an object?" I then told my client what I saw and she could only respond with, "My grandparents grew potatoes in their backyard, but I don't understand what it means." I decided not to go any further and the client went home. That was the first time a client did not make a connection with a spirit.

The next week, the same cold chill happened after the Reiki session with the same client. Again, I proceeded to explain what I saw. This time, however, I began to see an entryway in a house. I could see with great detail the doorway and the stairs. I was taking a virtual tour of this house! I could feel myself walking into the next room. There was a mirror on the wall which reflected a window with a shade. I realized I was very small, like a child, as I had to look up to see the mirror. I was too short to see myself. Also, I noticed that there was a stale smell to the air in the house.

The next room I walked into was the kitchen. I could see the entire layout and described it in great detail to my client. Then suddenly, I realized I was hiding behind a blue, checkered curtain used under the sink in the kitchen. I could feel a dampness on the floor as I trembled with fear. I heard my name being called and then saw two older people looking quite upset.

At that moment, I knew why they were upset. This child found their liquor.

I turned to my client and saw that she was sobbing. She began to tell me I had described the house where she had to live with her grandparents for a while when she was very little. She always felt they hated her. She also told me that they were alcoholics. I then told her that the message I was getting from them was that they did not know how to care for her but loved her very much. They were afraid she would get hurt. She then told me that they would punish her by putting her in the root cellar with the potatoes.

My client began to feel a tremendous sense of relief and stated that the pain from the temporal mandibular joint disorder in her jaw was gone for the first time in a long time.

My feeling is that I had somehow tuned into the client's energy vibration in the aura, with the help of her grandparent, where the healing was needed the most. This is quite different than the client experiencing a memory by way of self-hypnosis.

The following session demonstrates how self-hypnosis can be used in healing by incorporating the aura.

Self-Healing
May 1, 2003

I saw Mary today. She told me it is time to heal myself. She explained that in order to heal my sore right hand I need to see its energy in front of me detached from my body. Surround it with a bright white light while visualizing it as perfectly well and healed. Then allow the energy to go back to my physical hand. I can do this to any part of my body. I should do this often. I noticed that as I did this, I became extremely hot all over. My hand also twitched a bit. Something was happening. What a birthday present!

While in the state of hypnosis, Mary's approach to self-healing is uniquely different from the Reiki method. A Reiki practitioner can promote self-healing by simply placing their hands on themselves and allow the Universal Life Energy to enter. The principle is the same as with any Reiki healing session. Both methods, I have found, Reiki and self-hypnosis, seem to work well in healing.

To become a Reiki practitioner an individual has to undergo an attunement. This is a process that connects the practitioner with the Universal Life Force enabling them to be a conduit for the energy to heal. The practitioner, therefore, never uses his or her own energy in the healing process.

There are three levels of Reiki. After the first level of instruction and attunement, the practitioner may begin healing themselves and others. During the second level teaching, the practitioner receives three Sanskrit symbols. One of the symbols is used for distance healing. The other two are emotional/mental and empowerment. The third level is attunement to the master/teacher level. After the third attunement, the practitioner may then teach all the levels and attune others.

To begin a healing session, the practitioner asks for protection and enlightenment from the Universal Life Force while focusing awareness in their hands thereby taping into the life force energy. The intention is of the utmost importance as the practitioner sends the intent for the client's highest good. That energy is then transferred to the client where their energy system places it where it is needed the most at that moment.

When a client asks me what they can expect to happen during a session, I explain that they may experience different sensations such as, warmth or coolness, tingling in the hands and feet, slight involuntary muscle twitches, a slight sense of vibration, floating sensation, or nothing at all. I may or may not touch them and I always ask permission. It is very relaxing, simple, subtle and noninvasive.

CHAKRAS

This section of the chapter simply explains what Chakras are and their use in conjunction with Reiki. The word, Chakra, is Sanskrit and means "wheel" associated with the function of a vortex of spinning energy, passing through our bodies, influencing all of our bodily functions. Our bodies have seven main Chakras. Each is associated with color, sound and organ systems.

Chakras need to be in balance in order to maintain good physical health. As I mentioned earlier, the aura is the first defense against illness in the physical body. Chakras are based on frequencies and vibrations in the aura.

I was taught that each Chakra is associated with a color. If you look at a prism with the light shining through it, you will see the color spectrum. The colors are created by a distinct wave frequency vibrating the atom electrons passing through the prism. The Chakras vibrate to these same frequencies.

Each Chakra is associated with a musical note. As with

light, a sound is comprised of frequency and vibration. Sound therapy has been used for healing for a long time. There is evidence that the Egyptians formed their burial chambers to resonate with certain sounds to enhance healing. It would certainly make sense to me that energy vibrates at certain frequencies and we are energy as well as matter, therefore, we all must have an individual frequency and vibration that is very much like a fingerprint. No two are alike.

So, it is established that frequency and vibration are factors in color and sound but how are they connected to a Chakra? Perhaps this is one way to look at it. The color red is associated with the first Chakra energizing the bones and bone marrow. Bone marrow produces our blood and blood is red. It is one of the main structures of our body, therefore, connecting us to earth.

The musical note C is also connected to the first Chakra and its vibration and frequency resonate within the organ systems associated with that Chakra. Try saying the "C" note out loud and elongate the sound. You will notice it reverberates in the area of the first Chakra. Then try the other notes associated with each Chakra.

While writing this portion of the chapter, I came upon something rather interesting that I never gave a thought to previously. Musical notes can be matched to the same frequency and vibration of colors. Apparently, the note, C, for instance, is equal to the color green. If you will look at the note and color of the first Chakra, they are C and red. It appears that the note and color would not match.

I explored a little further and discovered that all the colors associated with each Chakra have a *contrasting* color that vibrates with the frequency of the musical note associated with a Chakra. For instance, the musical note C in the first Chakra vibrates to green not red. The color red vibrates to G flat, not C. I checked the colors of the other Chakras and the same holds true.

I, therefore, conclude that each Chakra must vibrate to two separate frequencies rather than one as I had previously been instructed. I believe that these two frequencies combined harmonize each Chakra. I am sure there will be those who will beg to differ with my conclusion, but it makes sense to me.

The bottom line is that Reiki practitioners use Chakras to bring harmony and balance to the energy system of the client, which then promotes healing and the sense of well-being. The Universal Life Force may not be seen by the naked eye, but the results are amazing.

The following is a list, as I was taught, of each Chakra and their corresponding colors and musical notes as well as parts of the body that are governed by each Chakra.

1. The first Chakra, or root Chakra, is located at the base of the spine. It governs the spinal column, bones, blood and teeth. It is associated with grounding, survival, safety and tribal connections. The color is red. The musical note associated is C.

2. The second Chakra, or Sacral Chakra, is located just below the navel. It governs the reproductive system, kidneys, adrenals and bladder. It is associated with creativity and life force. The color is orange and the musical note associated is D.

3. The third Chakra is located in the solar plexus just below the breastbone. It governs the stomach, gall bladder, liver, spleen, pancreas and nervous system. It is associated with self-empowerment. The color is yellow and the musical note associated is E.

4. The fourth Chakra is located over the heart. It governs the heart, lungs, thymus and circulatory system and is associated with love and compassion. The color is green and the musical note is F.

5. The fifth Chakra is located over the throat. It governs the vocals, thyroid and esophagus. It is associated with self-expression and communication. The color is light blue and the musical note is G.

6. The sixth Chakra, or third eye, is located between the eyebrows. It governs the lower part of the brain, pituitary gland, eyes, ears and nose. It is associated with intuition and intellect. The color is dark blue and the musical note is A.

7. The seventh Chakra, or Crown Chakra, is located six to twelve inches above the head. It governs the pineal gland and upper part of the brain. It is associated with spirituality, the higher self and the Universe. The color is violet and the musical note is B.

Chapter 5

The Visitor

Over the years I have recorded many journal entries of my visits to My Place, and my later entries suggest I have become more trusting of what I see and experience. It is clear to me that Mary was my guide, but I also have encountered other entities in My Place. Many times, Mary will tell me, "Someone is waiting to see you on the patio." Immediately, I find myself standing on the patio behind the Library. Sure enough, I am met with a familiar face, one of a deceased friend or family member. In the beginning I questioned some of the validity of these experiences. Was it just wishful thinking that I could see and converse with these loved ones? I was not thoroughly convinced until the day I was surprised by my visitor.

At the time, Joe and I had a small cottage on Cape Cod Massachusetts and our neighbors were Ted and Sandy from Connecticut. We both bought our cottages a year apart and became great friends. These cottages were part of an association and there was not much space separating the cottages. In fact, Ted and Sandy's cottage sat in front of ours about 15 feet away. We would end up looking at their bathroom window from our front deck. This became our common means of communication. We didn't bother with telephones. All we had to do was say, "Hey, Sandy, are you in there?" and she would come to the bathroom window. On weekends, whoever arrived at their cottage first, would have some lunch or snack to share. We always looked forward to our time together.

Joe and Ted were both very handy working well together on projects. Certainly, our little cottages required a great deal of attention from major remodeling to fixing a leaking pipe. Our other neighbors, at times, asked Joe and Ted to work in their cottages as well. It really was fun for them. They made a great team.

Several years ago, Ted had some bad news. He developed melanoma. He bravely fought hard but lost the battle. Joe and I knew that the end was near, but did not expect it that soon. Here is my story about my encounter with Ted's spirit.

It was a Tuesday morning when I was visiting My Place that Mary said, "Someone is waiting on the patio to see you." I could not believe it when I saw Ted standing there. I said, "Ted, what are you doing here?" He replied, "You can see me?" I said, "Yeah, I can see you." He said, "You can hear me?" I said, "Yes." He said, "No one else is listening!" I did not want to ask him if he had died because I did not want to hear the answer. I was not sure if I could trust what I was seeing. I then asked him to show me something to prove to me that he was real. He then showed me what looked like a green plaid-like bathrobe that he said was Sandy's. I had never previously heard either of them speak about the bathrobe. It seemed to be such a random object that I could have easily dismissed it as meaningless. I already was questioning Ted's visit in the first place. With that, I said, "Thank you." Then he disappeared.

At that point, I stopped the session and became concerned about Ted. I was not sure what to think. Had he died? I did not want to disturb Sandy not knowing if she was with Ted or sleeping. She was spending all her waking hours with Ted. She promised to call when she could so I thought I would just keep this visit to myself. A few hours later, Sandy called with the news that Ted had passed late the night before. I was hit with all sorts of emotions. I was saddened and felt it was not the time to share with Sandy what I experienced.

A few days passed and it was time for the funeral. Joe and I were the first ones to arrive. We built in extra travel time because we didn't know how long it would take to get to the funeral home in Connecticut.

After giving our condolences to the family, we sat in the second row facing the casket. People started streaming in which kept Sandy and her family quite busy.

As we sat, I suddenly had a feeling like someone was sitting in the empty seat next to me. Without warning, I heard Ted's voice say to me, "This is boring." I had all I could do to contain myself, but I did.

A few days later when I was checking in on Sandy, she asked if I had sensed Ted. She knew I was sensitive in that regard. Well, if there was ever a time to tell her, I thought, this was it.

I told her about the visit in My Place and the green bathrobe. There was a slight gasp on the other end of the phone. She said that Ted always told her that the green bathrobe was big enough to fit the two of them. The green bathrobe was a private joke between Ted and Sandy. This was another validation for me.

Then, I decided to tell her what I thought I heard Ted's voice say to me at the funeral home. She laughed and stated that every funeral they went to, Ted would say that it was boring! Well, we both got a little chuckle out of that story.

A few years later, Sandy told me what a great comfort she felt remembering what I had told her of my experiences with Ted's spirit. She knew in her heart that he was okay and would always be near.

My encounter with Ted's spirit never gave rise to any feeling of fear or creepiness that I might be hearing from someone who died. Certainly, it was not a scary feeling. In fact, I would say it seemed like the most natural thing in the world. He always had good positive energy. I can only hope for another visit from Ted someday.

Chapter 6

The Library

The first room I explored in My Place was the Library as described in Chapter 2. This massive Library houses all the books that I will be referencing. As you will see, there are even secret passageways in the Library. The room is full of surprises. For a long time, the Library was the only room I knew existed. It seems that my guide, Mary, would reveal new rooms and other places when she determined that I was ready to see them.

In the physical world, books are a part of my everyday life. So, in My Place what could be a more appropriate room than a Library? Also, I function better when organized, and a library epitomizes organization. This room is where I learned the skill of focusing. As far as I can remember, I have always been a dreamer and can get easily distracted. Practicing hypnosis has helped me to focus, but going to My Place has deepened my ability to focus even further.

After the first couple of years visiting the Library, I

believe Mary decided that it was time for me to explore beyond the books themselves.

Library Secrets
February 4, 2002

Mary greeted me today at the front door. I was surprised that I didn't find myself inside the room as usual. She said she thought I should know what the door looked like. I just didn't get it. She then said it was time for a tour.

I asked her if she could tell me more about the books in the Library. She said, "These books hold the knowledge of the Universe in this moment, not past or future."

While I stood in front of the shelves of books, I noticed two areas that resembled doors hidden in the wall of books. The first was a small door and Mary warned me that if I should pass through it, I would not return. She opened it to show me and it just seemed like a swirling tunnel of light, very ominous appearing. Perhaps it is the future. I did not ask.

The other door, hidden in the bookcase, opened to a set of stairs leading up to another level behind the books. The physical appearance of the wooden stairs did not seem to match the grandeur of the room. They were very narrow and extremely worn. At the top of the stairs I turned to the left down a dimly lit corridor. It resembled the lesser-visited area of an old Library. The odor of old musty books permeated the air. As I looked to my left, I noticed very ancient looking books and scrolls covered in dust and cobwebs. I assume by its appearance that this section holds the knowledge of past civilizations and of the Universe itself.

At the end of the corridor she showed me another set

of stairs. Also, there was an old water elevator. I noticed the long ropes, which would be used to raise the elevator to the next floor. Although it was an old one, I asked if we could use it and, instead, she laughed and said that I needed the exercise. So, we used the stairs and stepped into a huge room. It was well lit with bookshelves that were about waist high. The room seemed to have no end in sight. The shelves were filled with books, which Mary explained, represent everyone's life, past, present, and future. There were people everywhere busy milling around tending to the books. She said they were workers, guides and teachers. When we went back to the Library, Mary said, "This is the room where only we meet. No one else has access." It is just referred to as the "Library." I thanked her for the tour.

The Library, I would discover, had little mysteries tucked into its walls. The small door, which appeared so ominous, was a little scary. I remember feeling like stepping back as though it would have the power to draw me into the swirling tunnel.

Viewing the other large, secret room behind the bookcase gave me a feeling of awe as my eyes stretched beyond only to see no end in sight of the vast storage of books. Perhaps that was a peek at the Akashic Records.

The Akashic Records, believed to be a part of the Universal Consciousness, are thought by many to contain the archive of knowledge of the Universe. Our individual soul consciousness is the complete awareness of who we are unhindered by the physical body. Prophets and seers have been known to get into a deep level of consciousness to obtain such information. Could it be possible that I had a glimpse of the Akashic Records? The hidden room of books and people working was so immense that I could only imagine myself as but a tiny atom in this Universe. I felt so insignificant in contrast to its enormity.

As demonstrated in the writing below, it seemed there were more stories to be revealed in this Library.

The Cave
May 17, 2004

I just paid another visit to Mary. This time she was standing in a doorway behind the books. I never saw this opening before. Anyway, she said to hold her hand and watch my head. It was a dark little corridor with a low ceiling, which could be claustrophobic. We walked a short distance into a cave-like structure deep in the earth. We came upon a narrow, rocky ledge and looking below, I could not see the bottom. I could not see anything but a bright luminous light. Then I heard a baby cry, which I thought was extremely strange. Mary explained that the baby was my earth mother. As an infant, my mother received the light energy from deep within the cave. When I was born, the light energy was passed onto me.

Mary then said, "The stars of Pleiades helped form earth. The Pleiades constellation could no longer sustain life as the eighth star of the constellation exploded. All the energy from the life forms of the star were then scattered throughout the Universe. So, the light source in the cave is some of this energy. That is why you receive energy through your feet instead of your head, which is more common, when you practice Reiki healing." She said, "You have been around for a long, long time and now it is safe to use your gifts. You are but one of many whose energy originated in Pleiades."

We then went back to the room and she closed the corridor by sliding the bookcase over it. I felt safe back in the room. I thanked her.

This particular journal entry seemed like quite an extraordinary story to me. It sounded very much like an ancient myth. Mary had a way of explaining things to me by way of a story so that I could understand an idea on a deeper level. When you think about it, isn't that how Jesus preached to the people of his time? To make a point, he spoke of happenings in a parable that the people could relate to in their everyday lives. To me, the symbolism of the story is valuable. Certainly, this story, "The Cave," seems too farfetched to fit into the parameters of what physics has shown us to be fact. Or is it?

I think the lesson from this story is a symbolic representation and has to do with healing and understanding that healing comes from deep within our souls, from our very essence, our strength. This understanding has been passed from generation to generation, the stronger our commitment to heal, the better the results. Let the Universal Light within us shine through. We all carry this light. I believe mine comes from the earth.

There was one more surprise for me in the Library as described in the following entry.

The Little Black Box
May 16, 2004

"The truth will be revealed to you soon. Rewards are found after work and after demise."

Today I found this note tucked up underneath the top of the "little black box." I had not seen it before so I carefully peeled it off. I will try to explain the black box. A while back I asked Mary about a disembodied woman's voice I heard many years ago. Mary said that the woman left a "gift." She showed me a little rectangular black box. The finish was a shiny, lacquered black. The trim was a scalloped, gold embossed design with a pearl in the middle. When I opened it, the inside of the lid was dome shaped and unfinished wood to which was attached the note.

Surprisingly, the first time I opened this box, geometric designs of all sorts came out and surrounded me. I could smell the essence of flowers and herbs. I could hear musical notes. Mary told me it was healing energy. Anytime I want, I can open the box and I will receive this gift. I have also learned that I can share this energy with my clients for healing. Certainly, this place I go to in my mind is full of surprises.

In my Reiki practice, I have used the symbols from the box and remembered the musical notes and the multitude of fragrances. So, as I work with my clients, in my mind, I can open the little black box and allow healing energy to flow through.

The Library of my mind is full of wonderful surprises. Each time I visited the Library I was eager to explore my surroundings and feel the positive energy. Every experience was unique and every book was unique. Next, I will introduce the books, as they were shown to me.

Chapter 7

The Books

Now I will begin describing some of the books that I have come upon in this massive collection in the Library. As mentioned earlier, each book was unique in its physical appearance and the content was always a surprise.

The book covers were usually impressive whether it be the color, texture or material makeup. The titles were quite blatant like, "Book of Faith." Indeed, I found these books to be very strange and as I said, I never knew what to expect. Sometimes the books were not completely clear in my mind, so I learned how to focus. It has not been easy to learn that skill, but now I can apply it more in my everyday life.

I found the information within the books to be very cryptic in nature. Most of the time I ended up saying to my spiritual guide, Mary, "I don't get it!" Then, Mary would explain everything so that I would understand. At times I noticed Mary's frustration with me, but for the most part, she exhibited great patience.

One of the first books I remember viewing is described in Chapter 10, "The Gallery." It is titled, "Secrets of The Heart." It is a very key book, as you will see. However, the other books are described as follows.

Book of Many Lives
April 4, 2000

As mentioned in Chapter 3, I spent some time with my friend, Cyd, in her office discussing my experiences. We thought it might be interesting if she taped a hypnosis session. I found it very difficult to speak and keep up with what was happening in my mind, but I did my best. The following is the unedited transcript that Cyd recorded and transcribed.

Time: 12:25:40--Jan closes her eyes. 12:26:20--she moves her head. (Total of 40 seconds)
"I'm already on the path. Feet are bare and legs are bare from knees down." 12:27:25-" In the room. (Sigh) I found a green book. I just noticed that instead of the usual gold gilding on the edge of the pages, it has a brown or black edge, an almost burned look. I have to ask permission to open it and read it. Hm-m-m! It's strange. It's almost like I have an audience around me, almost like they are there to protect me. (Pause) I think I'm ready. (Sigh) 12:30:40 It's two columns. (Pause) Boy, it's going to take a few pages to get through this (Pause) OK! (Pause) it's innocence. Hm-m-m! (Smiles) I know why the book has black around it. It's old. Been through a lot. (Pause, moves head) It's just nothing I can decipher. No real words. Pages are so thin, I'm afraid I'm going to rip something. I can hear the pages as I turn them. Paper feels soft like velvet,

but it's not thick like that. Writing is almost like charcoal as if it's been burned into the pages. That's weird. (Sigh, pause) Ah, that was all I can see. That's a good start. Kind of boring, but all I can see."

"Now I want to see the red book next to the green book. I just realized the contrast in color, red versus green. See the pages. It says, 'Notes and Journals.' Pages are blank. There are no lines. I just realized some of the pages are in Chinese and other pages are in other languages. I promised myself I would try to see symbols. It's an effort to even try to get the pencil." (Picks up pencil and with eyes still closed begins to draw symbols on paper.) (Sighs, stops, looks tired, gasps for breath. Face to her right. Slowly rolls her head to upright and to her left.)

"I guess I'm tired. I have to put the book away cause I'm too tired. Um. I want to lie down on the couch to go to sleep. They say that's OK to do that but I can't now. (Pause, sigh) OK." (Jan opens her eyes at 12:42:15. Total time, 15 minutes, 55 seconds) "Wow!"

I need to fill in more details as I had trouble speaking during the session. I just knew this dark, hunter green colored book was the book that recorded my many past lives up to the present moment. There were two columns on each page. The left-hand column recorded every breath I took and thought I had. The right-hand column recorded what I had to learn from that living experience. The burned edges of the pages and the seared words indicated the permanence of each moment of time recorded in this book. The book appeared to be quite ancient and very fragile. The pages were as thin as onion skin paper and as I turned each page, I could feel the stiffness and hear the crackle as if it were old parchment paper.

The red book was interesting but, at the time, I did not ask its significance. Could this red book be the book that recorded my writings from other past lives? Are the blank pages in the red book titled, "Notes and Journals" being filled as I write this book? It is certainly a mystery.

The green book and its seeming permanence have had an impact on my present life in that I must realize and pay attention to all my thoughts and activities. I believe every thought and action we take leaves an imprint on our soul. Perhaps the more positive we are in life will be reflected like a mirror when we view ourselves at the end of our lives.

Book of Humor
August 29, 2001

It was the summer of 2001. My daughter, Ann Marie, had graduated from college in June and got married two weeks later. A week after the wedding my mother fell and broke her hip. It was going to be a tough recovery as she was already in her 80's, mostly deaf and legally blind. She lived by herself in a one-story, ranch style home. I would attend to her needs but for the most part, she really had done well on her own up to that point. Mom and I had a good relationship and she was mentally as sharp as a tack. However, because of her disabilities, and, now a broken hip, things were going to be different for a while.

She was very upset to think that she would have to go to the dreaded nursing home for a recovery period of several weeks. I could see it in her eyes and her voice. I could not do that to her. Consequently, the decision was made to care for mom at our house. Joe, being the angel that he is, thought it was a good idea. Mom seemed happy and relieved.

Here is my story and journal of what happened when I reached the end of my rope.

It was a very hot, seemingly long summer. After a short time with us, it became apparent that Mom and I were getting on each other's nerves. After about eight weeks of recovering from a broken hip, Mom went home in a huff. I guess she had enough of me and I her. When Joe and I were out, she demanded my daughter, Michele, drive her home immediately. I didn't think Mom was quite ready but she sure did.

Her time with us, let me just say, was not easy for any of us. All the worry, anxiety and stresses caught up to me in a physical manifestation. I developed severe hives and even a trip to the Emergency Room for my notorious, yearly, Labor Day weekend asthmatic attacks, being the height of the ragweed season. To say the least, I was a bit of a mess. I found myself at 2:00 a.m. in my family room cradling a box of tissues, feeling totally sorry for myself and worried about mom being home alone.

Since no one was awake at that hour, I could not vent to my poor family. Instead, I thought I could try to calm myself down visiting My Place, thinking, "Surely, Mary will listen with a consoling ear."

Somehow, I managed to quickly reach my destination of the Library despite my extreme anxiety. There I was, sitting in Mary's "office" as she called it with a smile. I asked her for help and she showed me the books and said, "Help yourself." I believe there was a double meaning in that remark.

I walked over to the books that reached floor to ceiling and stretched across the entire room. I began to focus on them when I noticed a lime green, colored book partially protruding from the shelf. I brought it over to the settee that faces the enormous stone fireplace. Mary told me to open the book titled, "Book of Humor." I remember thinking, how odd a title for this situation.

Upon opening the book, I was shocked to see that it really was just an empty box! Then from the box, I realized I heard what sounded like a laugh track from a TV situation comedy where the audience was getting a good chuckle. It blew me away for a second and all I could think was, "How absurd for Mary to show me a book like this at a time like this." I felt a slight rush of anger. After all, what I was going through certainly was not funny.

I then said, as usual, "I don't get it!" Mary explained to me the total absurdity of MY situation. I had managed to turn my emotions into a physical, wheezing, itching, manifestation. Isn't it amazing how I had wasted my precious energy? I guess it was a little absurd after I thought about it.

The lesson is, if I can learn to recognize an emotional reaction to a situation before it becomes a physical manifestation of sorts, then perhaps I can help prevent illness from emerging.

I always have heard that laughter is the best medicine. Sometimes we humans are not able to see any humor in our own situation. We really take ourselves too seriously. I had to step out and let someone much wiser show me, by way of the symbolism of the Book of Humor, just how poorly I handled my emotions. I let them get the best of me.

I also learned that sadness is so heavy it feels like

concrete taking over our energy. Humor is light and frees us to fill with life giving energy. Even by writing this, I am releasing the weight of stress.

I do have to see the humor in myself even though it may not always be easy. So, I guess I will have to refer to this journal as a reminder of how to handle the difficulties and absurdities in life.

The point of this writing was so powerful and the message so clear that every time I read it, I am amazed how I came to such a realization of the absurdity of my self-pity in the span of 15 minutes. I sincerely do not believe that I could have come to the same conclusion by any other means in that short time especially considering my agitated state of mind. Such an important lesson learned.

Book of Life
February 13, 2003

This morning I decided to visit Mary again. As usual, I first prayed for protection and enlightenment. I reached my destination quickly. I felt very happy and just wanted to talk to Mary but with no focused question. I asked her for a hug and as I did, she showed me her heart. I was quite surprised. It looked like multiple little daggers piercing her heart. She told me to remove one of the daggers. I didn't want to but she asked me so I complied. Immediately, I noticed her heart was bleeding. She then took my hand and placed it over the wound to stop the bleeding. As I did, she then said, "Go heal others." She explained that her heart bled in sadness for the events in the world that will be happening. I asked what I could do and *she simply said to love all.*

Then I asked her if there were any books she wanted me to see. We went to the shelves and she said, "Focus." I did and an apricot colored book was the one I chose. She said that I already possessed all the knowledge in the books but I need to be reminded. I went to the sofa and she sat next to me. I focused again on the book. It had no title on it. I opened it and it seemed the pages were there but only partly visible. I therefore, grabbed what seemed like a group of pages and fanned them all at once, which then revealed words or symbols on the partially visible pages. The faster the pages turned, the more solid they appeared.

This was very much like how a movie is made. If you look one frame at a time, it makes little sense but faster, you get the whole picture. She told me this book is the "Book of Life."

I guess we have to go through each day like one movie frame at a time and after the life is over, we can see the life like the full movie. Then there is clarity. Even the fact that the book had no title written on it says you won't find out what the book was about until the end after you fan the pages.

I thanked Mary for showing me this and asked her what I could give in return for these experiences with the books. She asked me to write a book. Okay.

Viewing Mary's heart was totally unexpected. Although she showed me a physical looking heart, I believe it was symbolic for the emotions of the heart. It made me understand how precious life is and how much healing has to take place in the world. It jarred me into realizing I had work that needed to be done. I thought that maybe by putting words on paper, the experiences I had in My Place would have a positive effect on whoever reads them. Certainly, this was the first time I thought about writing a book. The mere suggestion seemed like a daunting task especially since I did not consider myself a writer.

In the past, Mary had requested these sessions be recorded for future reference. Up till then, I only thought about writing a personal journal not for publication. Anyway, as usual, Mary was correct. If I did not write each session down, I would not remember everything and probably miss something important. As it was, many sessions went unrecorded for various reasons.

As far as the "Book of Life" goes, I find it interesting that I viewed this book on only its physical attributes rather than its content. I didn't see words clearly. I believe that Mary meant to show me only the symbolism of the "Book of Life."

Many times, we hear people say, "I saw my life flash in front of my eyes." It usually occurs when someone thought they were going to die suddenly. Maybe they then realized how short life really is. Our time on earth is very quick when compared to cosmic time. I hope someday I will see my "Book of Life" again. Perhaps next time I will see its contents.

Book of Purpose
March 21, 2003

I believe that every life has a purpose. Some of us spend all our lives trying to find our main life purpose. My advice is to stop wasting time searching and just go about your life. Your purpose will find you. We tend to narrow things down to one generalized purpose in an effort to simplify. I also believe every life has more than one purpose. If you think about it, every day and every moment have a purpose even if it seems insignificant. You don't know how you affect other people by a gesture or a kind word.

Sometimes a person's life purpose continues after they die. Think about all the foundations and organizations that are named after an individual who has passed, especially children who died way before what we think should have been their time. They are usually remembered for the disease that caused their demise or crime that was committed against them. The foundations and funds set up in their names help cure diseases or help protect others from dangerous criminals. Everyone's purpose is as diverse as the individuals themselves. The following is a description of my "Book of Purpose."

I visited Mary again. I noticed that where her face should be under the hood was empty and dark. It seems that whenever there is great turmoil in the world the light is gone.

She held my hand as we stood in front of the books. She took out a purplish black book. She said it was the book that told me who I really was and my purposes. It was the "Book of Purpose." The pages were a grayish color with gold writing that I could not read. She told me to place my hand on each page and the information would be absorbed.

I learned my main purpose is to help people to spiritually reconnect with the Universe and that I am a "Soldier of the heart." I must not fear death or evil. Evil is really the lowest form of human life, which needs to be understood and shown the light. Fear of anything is of no use. It has no purpose other than to destroy. My strongest Chakra is my heart that is always connected to the Universe. I must guard it carefully. I will see things when I am ready. I have a big job ahead of me.

I suppose after having viewed the "Book of Life" a few weeks earlier it was only natural to want to know about my purpose. I felt very good about this book.

Absorbing the information instead of reading the words made sense to me in a strange sort of way. Sometimes words fall short of relaying a message, whereas absorbing the energy of the book is more visceral and the meaning is crystal clear. I like knowing that I am a "Soldier of the heart."

Book Etched in Stone
March 28, 2003

I asked Mary if we come from the stars. She took me to the books. High on the top shelf, which I could not reach, was the book. She told me to project myself up to the shelf. As I did, I looked down on her and myself. I thought, "How strange." I took the book and returned to my normal self. The book appeared multicolored in greens and blues and looked like the glaze on the pottery piece I made in art school, the one that "Didn't come out right." The one that looked old, heavy and pitted. The book suddenly felt heavy like a block of stone. It was stone!

All my questions were answered at that moment. Our existence is etched in stone. We all come from the energy light of the stars. The stars are made from the elements and we are too.

I felt so small. Then I said, "My part in this world seems so tiny." Mary reminded me how one stone thrown into a pond can cause the ripple effect and spread far and wide long after the stone has disappeared from sight. Well, I may not be creating a tsunami, but I understand we all possess the power to change things, big or small. The book is solid stone and meant to last.

Mankind's existence on earth always seems threatened either by wars, disease or natural disasters. But, remember, we are energy and energy cannot be destroyed. No matter how minute our actions or thoughts may seem to be, there is an effect somewhere. Our thoughts can affect our mood that can be felt and transferred to someone else and so forth. So, be careful what you think or do. You may be more powerful than you realize.

Of note, it seems that during March of 2003, I journaled quite a bit. There must have been a full moon! Each time I went to My Place, it was very enlightening as with this next journal.

Book of Death
March 30, 2003

Mary was waiting for me. It was a beautiful day. I put my arm around her as we walked outside and sat down at the table on the patio. She told me it was time to see the "Book of Death." I was afraid. She said, "People who say they are not afraid of death are 'whistling in the dark' unless they have had a near-death experience, which seems to alleviate all their fears." Even so, I think we all have some degree of fear, mostly of the way we will die or the thought of leaving everyone behind. Mary said, "People lose the fear at the time of death because that is when they see the truth, and, therefore, no longer have fear."

Reluctantly, she handed me the book. The cover reminded me of yin and yang, black and white intermingled close together. She said, "Death is harmony. It is the peace and understanding but not the end. It is simply change and transition." Life and our spirits still exist in the light. Only our bodies are in the dark in death. One needed the other to exist in physical form. Now the light is free and unburdened by the body.

I learned that when someone we love dies, some of our light leaves us, which creates our sadness. Each time we have good memories of our loved ones, we receive some of our light back again. I did not open the book.

Death is a hard subject for most people to discuss. As Mary said, "Apparently those who have experienced a positive near-death no longer fear death as they have had a glimpse of what is to come." That thought can help remove the fear for some people. Certainly, no one wants to leave their loved ones on this earth, but it would be nice to know that we reunite with others who have passed before us knowing someday the ones left behind will also join us.

The purpose of this journal is not to cause fear about death but understand that death is really about change. I believe that we, our consciousness, continues to exist with our memories stored in our soul's energy. I also believe that our brains do not create consciousness. Instead the brain is the vehicle for our consciousness to function in the physical world. So, to me, it only makes sense that we, our consciousness, should continue beyond physical death as we transition into another form of existence. I think if I should come upon the "Book of Death" again, I will welcome the chance to open the book.

Book of Self-Healing
May 5, 2003

*When I visited My Place today, Mary looked puzzled or worried and thought I had a strange request. I wanted to learn more about self-healing. I guess she thought I already knew. She showed me the books and I focused to find one that stood out. It was a beautiful yellow book with a gold design on the cover. She told me to take it out onto the patio where my brother was waiting for me. (*From my Catholic background, I saw him as Jesus) *He told me to open the book to the first chapter. On the first page I saw pictures of snakes, mice and other small animals. This first chapter was about instinct, knowing truth, and the nature of survival. The next chapter was about responsibility, acceptance and to act on this knowing, inner truth. Take responsibility for my own health. Accept who I am. Embrace knowledge and truth, as it is necessary for my healing and survival.*

I think the Book of Self-Healing was a reminder of how I don't pay enough attention to my physical body to keep it healthy. Perhaps we all become dependent on technology to keep us healthy like body scans and pharmaceuticals. So many things in our environment hamper our natural instinct for maintaining good health.

For instance, when it comes to food there have been times I have fallen short of good instincts. In general, I believe fast food, in all forms, such as, highly processed convenience foods, and chain restaurants have helped destroy our health. This is only one example of not taking responsibility for our own health. The knowledge and truth about our food is often distorted and confusing. The responsibility still lies with us to seek out the best food for our bodies. Hippocrates said, "Let food be thy medicine." He was so right. It seems that pills prescribed for conditions such as diabetes or heart disease are really permission slips to continue eating unhealthy foods.

I thought about why I feel guilty after eating cookies or fast food that I know are bad for me. It is my instinct telling me, "Do not eat it", and I have just disobeyed. I guess the lesson is, pay attention to my instincts and take responsibility caring for myself. The knowledge and truth reside within me so I need to listen to that little voice inside my head when it tells me right from wrong.

Book of Relaxation
January 11, 2004

I visited Mary today before I got out of bed this morning. I wanted to tap into her great wisdom to find a way for me to release anxiety and stress. I seem to manifest stress in different areas of my body that consequently cause me discomfort, therefore, creating more stress. It reminded me of the time I took care of mom a few years ago with her broken hip.

Stress, what a waste of energy! Anyway, Mary told me it's my basic personality and DNA to easily get stressed out. That sounded like an excuse. I guess it really means I have to work harder at conquering stress.

I looked at those marvelous books on the shelf and a furry looking one caught my eye. I looked at Mary and she gave me a gesture indicating this was the book to take out. At first, I was not sure about touching it because I did not know what that furriness might be. As I pulled the book off the shelf, I noticed it felt silky smooth and more strand-like than furry. It was a golden color. It was corn silk! A book covered in corn silk. How bizarre! Of course, all these books in this Library could be described as bizarre.

I opened it. She said it was the Book of Relaxation. It contains things I like and enjoy, past, present and future. These things make me happy and when I'm happy, I'm relaxed. She reminded me I can't prevent stresses in my life but these things will help me handle difficult situations a little better.

The first page had sheet music to symbolize my love of music. Then much to my surprise, I saw many pages containing pictures of paintings. I believe some were paintings from the Gallery but many more were there. These are my future thoughts of paintings that either will become my finished works or just ideas. Beyond the paintings were other fun things I like to do including Reiki, and cooking, karate, etc. As I touched the corn silk, I remembered how I used to like to play with it as a child. It had a calming effect on me.

I have fond memories as a child on a hot summer day of my father picking some corn from the garden. I loved the warm sweet smell of the sun-drenched ear of corn, as I was about to husk it. For some reason, the corn silk was my favorite part. When I would touch it, the softness always relaxed me. It seemed in contrast to the hardness of the cob to which it was attached. I remember mixing the corn silk with the mud pies under the old apple tree in the back yard. I guess I liked cooking even back then. Maybe the simple things in life really do give the greatest pleasure. As Mary once said to me, "Simplicity leads to completeness."

Book of Crystal
December 6, 2004

I decided to visit Mary today. Some time has elapsed since I last journaled. A couple of weeks ago I had asked Mary about my mom's future demise, as it seems eminent now that the doctors say things can't be fixed as far as her blood pressure and arteries are concerned. Mary had told me I would lose my mom before the next full moon, but I still have her so I have begun to distrust in these sessions. Yet, such profound things had been experienced during my sessions that I feel confused, not fully trusting in them anymore.

The first time I went back to My Place last week, I noticed the Library smelled like it had been cleaned and I could not see Mary. Instead, as I turned around, I bumped into a very tall being, hooded so I could not see his face, but I recognized him, as seen in my mind, being present at a couple of Reiki sessions. He said I was not allowed to come back until I trusted again.

He said that I misinterpreted what Mary meant when she said that I would lose my mother by the next full moon. As I thought about it, Mary was right. Over the last few weeks Mom has changed dramatically. She really is not the same person. She is more accepting of her coming demise. Her bitterness is not noticeable to me anymore. She only wants peace. Because I now believe that is what Mary meant, I decided to try to go back to My Place and look for her.

I found her by the books and asked her to show me a book to help me understand. I began to focus on the shelf of books and waited to see if one caught my eye. It did. It showed like a jewel. The book is covered in a crystal type of material and iridescent. Mary said this stone couldn't be found on the surface of the earth in that form but it exists deep inside. When it comes to the surface as molten lava, cools and mixes with the air, it is changed so you can't see its original form. This book is covered with its original form. It has, therefore, a priceless value. It is what we have all come from. It holds the elements of life, all forms. I have much to learn from this book. The energy of crystals is real. Because I do not understand crystals, I have had great reservations about them. Mom has simply returned to her original form of kindness and understanding.

This book symbolizes change. My mother had a hard life from the day she was born. Her mother died during her childbirth and her father became so distraught that he could not take care of her. She was brought up by her father's parents and occasionally an uncle or aunt. I think it is fair to say that her childhood was tough. She also suffered from multiple ailments throughout her life. So, by looking at her background of hard knocks, it would be reasonable to assume that was why she was unhappy in life.

However, having received the news from the doctor that she was not going to last much longer, she began to reflect on her life. I guess when we are told that our deadline is closing in fast, we start to look at what is really important to us. Call it mellowing out if you want. So, I believe, as the crystal book demonstrates, that we come into this world in a certain physical form and personality. Our exposure to the elements of time and environment can cause us to change. It may take the sudden realization of our own mortality to make us stop and reevaluate our lives and again be whom we were when we came into this world. Perhaps when we pass, we return to our original form. This makes sense to me.

Book of Family
November 1, 2005

I visited Mary and asked if I could be shown things that will help our family. She showed me another book. It was a beautiful dark blue, sort of indigo, with gold on the page edges. The pages were of the purest white. It was called, "Book of Family" on the outside cover.

The first page had a massive, blood red spot in the middle that spread out from the center like little spider veins. The other pages that followed almost to the end of the book had less and less red until there was finally a clear page near the back of the book. Mary said the blood was from everyone's broken heart that has spilled and joined to form the spot. Time will eventually fade away the blood as if the pages of the book were blotters. The more pages, the less absorbed until finally, the last page is clean.

I guess it may take a very long time to blot away the blood that was spilled. Maybe since the blood has already been spilled and the damage has been done, no more injury can be inflicted. Healing can begin. I hope so. I am saddened that some of that blood was mine, as I felt powerless to help the situation.

When writing this book, I was uncertain whether I would include this entry as it seemed so personal and, yet, there are so many other families that suffer the consequences from misunderstandings leading to family dysfunction. Perhaps you know one. It does not seem to matter about the socioeconomic background as it can affect any family.

The Book of Family is symbolic of the pain and suffering that poorly executed words can cause. The blood spot spreads outward into smaller veins in the paper that could be seen as representing other family members having nothing to do with the original disagreement. As a family member, I too have been affected; therefore, I symbolically bleed from sadness. Each page following the red spot represents time and eventual healing.

Chapter 8

Spirit, Soul and Karma

Spirit and Soul

As mentioned in the introduction, I found it difficult to understand the difference between spirit and soul. When I reference "spirit", I am talking about the part of our soul that is closest to God, the Highest Power of Good or however you reference positive energy. It is life itself. The word, "soul" is used in reference to the energy that is closest to our body. As I stated in the Introduction, I believe our soul is our personality and who we really are which is spiritually connected to others comprising Universal Consciousness. For instance, when a child is conceived, a soul enters the fetus which is then connected to the life-giving force of Spirit. In other words, our spirit, is the life energy that fuels the physical body and soul. Since the words, spirit and soul, are often used interchangeably, it can be confusing.

It appears that in modern everyday language, the

word, spirit, is loosely thrown around. It can imply how someone is feeling, such as being, "high-spirited" meaning having a lot of energy. There is "free-spirited" which indicates that a person will do whatever they want. "Weak-spirited" describes someone who does not have much of a backbone and lets people walk over them. The opposite is "mean-spirited", probably the one who does the walking over the weak-spirited person. However, these interpretations of spirit only define the level of energy exhibited by an individual.

Many times, the word, spirit is also used interchangeably with the word, ghost. To simplify and clarify, a ghost is perceived as not having passed to the next dimension and remains in the physical world. Ghost stories abound, some are true and others are scary only to be told around a campfire late at night in the middle of the woods or on Halloween. These stories tend to be over exaggerated and meant to cause a sleepless night for the unfortunate listener. Most ghostly disturbances are to be left in the category of the unexplained. It is believed that some psychics and mediums have the ability to help these spirits move on to the "light" in the next dimension. Once passed, they are free to interact with us and help guide us on our earthly journey.

Hope, faith, and will are all words that can be used to describe the frequency and vibrational strength of our spirit. We know that physical strength is not enough for our bodies to live forever, as the physical world will eventually reclaim its physical parts. Our bodies wear out, as I believe they are temporary vehicles for our souls.

As mentioned earlier in Chapter 4, I believe that our soul holds memory and continues beyond our death. For instance, in many cases of a near-death experience, after revival, a patient may report having viewed themselves from above their body. They were able to describe their exact circumstances and surroundings repeating word for word what medical personnel were saying while trying to revive the patient. Those present would validate the descriptions of what occurred for the entire time the patient was clinically dead. In many cases, there was no brain function to permit the ability to see, hear or remember what happened. Yet, the details reported could not be disputed. Therefore, it is my belief that our soul's consciousness stores memory and continues to survive after death.

Perhaps that is why past life regression hypnotherapy is so intriguing to me. Through the process of hypnosis, we are able to reach a point where there is communication between body and spirit. It is a fascinating process. Assuming my theory is correct that our spirit energy retains memory, it should explain how we could connect with memories from another lifetime. I have observed that some individuals who practice hypnosis are naturally better than others, but most people have some degree of success, much to their amazement.

My friend, Cyd, often refers to our bodies as "space suits." When we release the body, we release our ties to the physical world hopefully having learned from our experience on earth. Our spirits are but one tiny, yet, intricate part of the greater consciousness of the Universe.

It seems to me, based on my own experience with spirits, that they can come and go at will and have more insight that they would like to share with us. I can only imagine how frustrating it could be for them to try communicating with the living when we ignore their signs. Remember in Chapter 5, "The Visitor", Ted had just passed when I encountered him in My Place. He seemed surprised and relieved that I could see and hear him. I was taken aback by his sudden appearance having been unaware of his passing.

I believe when we die, our consciousness continues in our spirit. We no longer have the physical impairments that plagued us while alive. I believe our personalities do not change and we have access to knowledge that we could not have while in physical form. Next, since Mary has referenced karma in some sessions, I feel the need to discuss the subject.

Karma

What is Karma? Fundamentally it is cause and effect. There is the Eastern view and Western view. For instance, in the Western view if someone robs a bank and gets away with it, then loses the money, it could be viewed as bad karma. The robber has gotten what he deserved. If the robber never lost his money before he died of old age, having gotten away with it, maybe in the next life, he will meet with justice. The opposite is also true. If you do good things, good things will come to you. It seems to be a pretty straightforward way to look at karma.

The Eastern view of karma seems to be focused on the internalization of a wrongdoing. If someone robs a bank, there are immediate ramifications. The robber knows it is wrong even though he may justify it for his own purposes. However, on a subconscious level, he has to deal with the guilt of that action which, in time, may affect the robber in a negative way spiritually and psychologically. It will always be there in the back of his mind. If the robber has no conscience, I assume he will have to deal with it in the afterlife.

You don't have to rob a bank to create bad karma. Little things in life such as being a little mean to someone can be bad karma. Yelling at your kids or your spouse is creating bad karma. These acts come from selfishness. You had a bad day and you are taking it out on someone else.

We have choices to make every day and these choices determine what we learn. Free will is our gift to make choices. What we do with it can create good or bad karma.

So, imagine you are feeling bad about yelling at your spouse or kids. What are you going to do about it? Do you buy them a present and ask forgiveness? Do you do something nice for them? That sounds like a good thing to do, but are you really doing it to make *you* feel better? Can true remorse nullify the bad karma? They may forgive you, but you still have to deal with it in your head. See if you can forgive yourself. I think the best way to deal with bad karma is to try not to create any. However, we are human. Need I say more?

The next type of karma that I would like to discuss is karmic debt, which sounds very negative. Karmic debt is a buildup of karma, which needs to be paid back. It is associated with avoiding responsibilities. With regards to my experiences, this is what I have come to understand. The session below was the first time I encountered the idea of karmic debt.

Karmic Debt
November 10, 2003

I saw Mary again today. She said I have a karmic debt to pay the Masters, who I think must be spirits of an angelic nature. I didn't understand what she meant. She said they have given me many important gifts and I must use them. That is how I pay back my debt to them. They are expecting me to heal and paint. I am afraid if I fail, I may lose the gifts.

When you are given something important, the expectation is that you do something with it of equal importance. For instance, if someone gifted you the deed to a large corporation and you just did nothing, the corporation would probably fail. It needed your active involvement to keep it going. There are responsibilities attached to such a gift, therefore, you should feel indebted to succeed.

In my case, I feel that I have responsibilities to fulfill with regard to my gifts of healing and art. I believe everyone is born with certain gifts. Some are more obvious than others such as music or art. It is what we do with them that counts. If you use what has been given to you to your greatest potential, then you have fulfilled your obligation. The giver will feel happy that you respected and cherished the gift. If it is ignored, its value is worthless and the giver would be reluctant to give again. We, in turn, would miss out on the experience and opportunities of having the gift.

Many times, I have heard the question whether physical suffering is some kind of karmic payback for something we have done wrong in our life. The following session clarifies the answer.

More on Karmic Debt
May 8, 2007

I found Mary today and I could see her face clearly. She held my head in her hands and I began asking her questions. I asked her about my spinal disc problem. She said things may get worse and I might look at my present condition as nothing by comparison. I asked if suffering is karmic payback. She said, "Suffering physical or emotional pain is the Universe's way of forcing you to be in a position where you are unable to continue your life the way you have known it. It is time to see your suffering as an opportunity to change or do something different." Perhaps I should evaluate my karmic debt and take this opportunity to pay it back.

We are given gifts when we come into this world. If we don't use them we owe a karmic debt for having been given something special. To use our gifts repays the debt. This works for everyone. Instead of feeling sorry for myself, I have to get over being upset and angry. I must see this as an opportunity. If I can turn a negative situation into a positive one, then I have learned an important lesson. Hindsight is a great teacher. I will evaluate my options and look for my opportunities.

Mary was right. The pain in my back did become unexpectedly severe before surgery. The experience of this session made me stop and think about many things. Since I had time to spend recuperating, I evaluated my options including how to use my gifts wisely and not let them go to waste.

Chapter 9

More Books

It seems that the messages from the sessions I have received are not earth shattering in themselves. We all have heard similar adages such as, "let it go" or "forgive yourself". However, when I am in a deep state of hypnosis, these same adages become embedded in my subconscious. They carry more weight in their significance and, consequently, I have a deeper understanding of their importance. Certainly, the way I receive the insights is remarkable, but, for me, what is important still comes down to the messages I share from the books.

Book of Truth
December 8, 2005

I visited Mary again today as I felt the need to find the truth about a personal matter. Again, I found her standing near the books. I think she already knew what was on my mind. She pointed to the books, so I began to focus. However, this time something extremely strange happened. For an instant, all the books on the shelves popped out and then popped back into their original position. All I could think was how much it reminded me of a cartoon on TV where things like that happen.

I was a little bit startled so I turned away from the books. I was about to take a step when I almost tripped over a book that had apparently fallen from the shelf. Mary asked me to pick it up. As I did, I noticed that it was a heavy book with a slightly bumpy feel to the dirty cover. I say, "dirty" because the cover appeared to have been white, but, due to a great deal of handling, it was grayed in places. The front cover of the book said, "Book of Truth." I thought it was a strange way of presenting the book to me.

Mary suggested I sit in front of the fireplace to open the book. As I did, I could not help but feel a little nervous and excited. Upon opening the book, I noticed immediately, a perfectly round, large hole in the middle of the pages. It went straight through to the back of the book. There appeared to be words on the first page surrounding the hole but too blurry to read. Again, I looked at Mary and said, "I don't get it!"

Mary then explained to me that words could be expressed all around a truth but not give you answers. The hole in the book meant that the truth is a knowing. No words or pages are necessary. I already knew the truth. I just had to admit it to myself.

I thought it was interesting that I almost tripped over the Book of Truth. Sometimes the truth is right in front of our noses but we can't see it or don't want to see it. The book looked like it had been kicked around a few times being grayed and dirty. Probably this is symbolic for not paying attention and ignoring the truth like kicking it out of my mind. I believe the book represents my whole truth.

As far as truth being a knowing, I think we all have a little voice inside our heads that most of the time we don't pay enough attention. I'm learning to take the time to listen to myself think and I might be surprised what I will hear. I don't need a book to find my truth.

Book of Faith
January 4, 2006

I visited Mary again. She was pleased and I think I could see her face a little clearer. I saw her smiling. I could tell she wanted me to view another book. As I began to focus, I could see a book appearing as a lush, reddish brown, very rich in color with gold edges. The front cover had a slightly recessed circle with words in gold saying, "Book of Faith." She told me to focus very hard as I opened the book. The first page read, "Acknowledgements: To God and all who follow."

I turned another page and, again, just like the "Book of Truth," I saw a very large hole in the middle with a ragged, convoluted edge around the inside of the hole. She told me to smooth it around with my hand. I could not understand how I could smooth paper. As I touched it, I realized it was not paper but a clay-like substance that was pliable. Mary explained that faith is like a truth. No words are necessary. It is a knowing. The difference between the "Book of Truth" and this book is that truth is constant. It does not waiver. Therefore, the hole in the "Book of Truth" cannot be changed. However, the hole in the "Book of Faith," can be molded just as faith can be lost or gained. I guess my faith was a little rough around the edges and I needed to smooth it out a little.

I am not sure what I had lack of faith in, but I apparently worked it out at the time. Faith does not necessarily have to do with religion. Do you have faith in your loved ones, or yourself for that matter? Perhaps there may have been times when you doubted your own judgment or someone else's and lost faith.

Mary showed me the distinction between truth and faith in an interesting way. It was simple and straightforward. Truth is fact, therefore, unchangeable, proven beyond doubt. I think faith is belief based on emotions and perceived facts. If the facts are proven false, then faith is shattered.

Angels, for example, cannot be scientifically proven to exist. However, if you have had a mystical experience in which you believe you saw an angel, then you now have faith in angels and that faith becomes your truth. Someone else will hear of your experience and believe you, but because they have not experienced it themselves, they can only have faith that angels exist.

I am thinking how difficult it is to put into words exactly what I want to express as the difference between faith and truth. Yet, when Mary showed me the books, it was easier to understand the difference. I believe there are times that symbolism, as demonstrated in both books, does a better job of explaining than words. It helps substantiate the idea of "knowing" and that words are not necessary to convey a thought.

Book of Choice
January 13, 2006

I came across another important book today. It was the "Book of Choice." It is a relatively small black book with the yin and yang symbol raised on the front. I opened the book. The pages in the first half of the book were rather parchment-like and light rusty colored with what appeared to be a thin watercolor wash of blue. Then the other half of the book had a bright white paper with distinctive colored, amorphous shapes. I asked Mary, "Why?" She explained that I had a choice about how I was going to see. (At the time I found this book, I had great concerns about losing my eyesight in the future due to optic nerve problems.) *Was I only to see a darkened blur or the clear crisp lights and colors? It's up to me to decide. I chose the latter.*

Physically I may not have the choice but spiritually and emotionally I do have a choice. What I choose to see through my heart and mind is clarity. That guides direction. Direction guides progression so I would be able to get past any affliction with this choice. After all, I am not just a physical being with failing eyes. I can still see clearly if I choose.

Some people believe that we all have a predetermined destiny. Maybe we do, however, how we get there could be quite convoluted if you believe in free will. Free will means free choice to control your life. Maybe we are guided by a higher power, but, because of free will, we choose our own path. The path we choose may be smooth or full of obstacles. Sometimes, there is no easy way.

I believe, in the case of my possible future blindness, if

it should occur, I will accept my fate. Physically, I won't have a choice, but my spirit will continue to maintain clarity.

Book of Friendship
April 12, 2006

Christina's funeral is today so I felt I really needed to see Mary. I went to My Place with no expectation of what book I would be shown if any. Mary and I sat at a small table next to the books. She held my hands and warned me that the funeral for my friend was going to be more difficult than I was expecting.

I asked her if there were any other books for me to see today and she said to look and I would find it. I scanned the books and I saw one that had writing on the binding, which is unusual. It said FRIENDSHIP on a light blue background. I took it off the shelf and noticed the front and back covers were white with scattered words of encouragement and fondness. Then multiple colors began to appear on the cover changing and flowing into each other like a kaleidoscope. I didn't understand. Then Mary said, "The binding stays the same, as does the bond of a friendship. The colors represent emotional changes in the friendship over time. Even as you think of that friend, your thoughts may fluctuate from a good memory to one of sadness. Each side of the cover represents half of the friendship. A friendship may be very deep or shallow."

If I had opened the book, which I didn't, the real friendship would be revealed. Again, it's a truth. I hope to revisit the book and open it. It isn't time yet.

Recently I was reading this journal entry and realized

that the multiple words on the cover reminded me of a yearbook that is passed around and signed by classmates. Some are close friends while others are just acquaintances. I felt close to Christina.

After the funeral was over, I, and another woman I knew, were the first to leave. As we opened the door to exit the building, we were both surprised to see two large white butterflies in front of us flying around each other in a delightful dance then both flew over the top of the roof. The other woman with me said, "It's Christina!" My tears flowed like a river down my face. Then I suddenly realized that butterflies are not around this early in the season especially such a cold one. In the midst of my broken heart I sensed that she was saying goodbye. I felt peaceful and relieved knowing she was free at last from pain and suffering.

More on the Book of Family
April 26, 2006

Mary greeted me at the little brown table by the books. I thanked her for everything. I asked again about the family since we are in counseling. She showed me the "Book of Family", only this time, the part that was originally bright red blood had become chard black. She said it meant the wound, in essence, was cauterized to stop the bleeding which then means healing can now start. She mentioned death again. Death can mean either physical death or a change in circumstance. Death is a change any way you look at it. That is what will occur to change the family dynamics.

Since all the books in this Library are knowledge of the Universe in the present moment, they may not appear the *same each time I see them. Change is an important part of the Universe. As our earth travels through space, it meets with energy bombarding earth constantly, therefore, ever changing the world as we know it including our thoughts. So as the energy from vibrations and frequencies change earth, so does everything else change including thought. Thought allows free will to make choices and changes. I think if nothing changed, we would all probably die, as energy cannot sustain itself without frequency and vibration. Vibration is movement. Movement is energy. Maybe the energy change will be happening soon for the family so the frequency and vibration can affect family member's thinking and choices for the better. Please, Universe, help us out.*

I felt it was a shame that the counseling was unsuccessful as the parties involved could not come to terms. It was difficult to see those I loved unable to get past their differences.

Little did I know at the time I wrote this journal that in four years we would lose a dear family member at the young age of 64. It was very unexpected. The loss brought the realization to the family of how precious life is and what is really important, love.

Secrets of Body and Soul
September 8, 2006

Today a Mass was held at St. Mary's for Mom. It also happened to be the Feast of The Blessed Mary's Birth. Even the song they sang was Mom's favorite, Ave Maria.

I decided to go home and visit Mary. I found her and

wished her Happy Birthday. She said that everything was fine with Mom and Dad. I then asked her if there were any more books with secrets and she said, "Plenty." So, I looked at the books until one became prominent. It was an orangey, red book with gold edging. No words were written on the front, but the book felt very heavy. The binding said, "Volume I," and then lower down it said, "Secrets of Body and Soul." I didn't understand what this was about. I opened the book and a weird thing showed up. It was a real beating heart. I asked her, "What is the meaning?" She tried to explain that the heart is the connection between body and soul. When the heart begins to beat in a fetus, there is a soul, a mind. That is why the heart is one of the first organs to develop and start working completely.

Regardless, I bear a heavy heart today. I miss you Mom.

When doing bodywork, such as massage or Reiki, I am aware of a person's energy as well as physical body. The heart is considered to have the largest energy center, or Chakra, in the body. It reaches out from us the farthest. There have been many times I have noticed that a person has pulled their heart energy close to them even though they are totally unaware. I think on a subconscious level, they are protecting themselves. After a short time during their session, once they feel safe and secure, they allow that energy to reach out again.

Many years ago, I had a family member who would often come for either a massage or Reiki. He was so open all the time that I could tell the moment he walked in the door what was bothering him. He always said, "How did you know that?" Then, tragically, his twin brother, age 52, passed away from an illness. When that occurred, he said he felt part of him died. From that point on I was never able to reach him. He pulled all his heart energy inside. Unfortunately, six months later, he too suddenly passed away. Perhaps the lesson learned is that our emotions, in this case, extreme grief, may take away our life-giving energy and help create or hasten the progression of a preexisting physical ailment.

The body and the soul work together. I believe the heart is the seat of our emotions. The soul is the master controller and the body reacts accordingly. The secret is, knowing your own soul and body.

Book of Changes and Mary's Name
January 4, 2007

Today I visited Mary in the Classroom. (The Classroom is explained later in the book.) *It was a bright and sunny day this time. She told me that questions begin the learning process and it is knowing the right questions to ask. So, I asked her what her real name was. She said, "Names are just a personification of the spirit. You have a comfort with 'Mother Mary'. Therefore, if that is who you perceive me to be then that is who I am."*

On another subject, a client told me about Chi Kung and she mentioned the "Book of Changes." I did not ask her what it was about at the time but it piqued my curiosity so I asked Mary about such a book. We went to the Library. She handed me a book and said it was a version of the "Book of Changes" I could understand. She put her arm around my shoulder as if to protect or comfort me. I opened it to see what appeared to be a video.

The video showed life cycle changes of flesh decaying

to bones then nourishing the land. It demonstrated how chi energy is recycled so balance is maintained by constant change. Therefore, constant change equals constant life. It's a simple concept.

All energies must have negative and positive chi to be balanced and healthy. Then there is harmony. So, negativity is actually okay as long as it is balanced with positivity. Circulation of chi is change.

My friend, Cyd, asked me one day how I knew that my guide, Mary, was "Mother Mary." I told her that she looked the way I would think Mother Mary would appear. She always wore a blue, rough woven hooded robe with white trim. Most of the time her face was very bright but there have been a few times I could see her more clearly. She has olive colored skin, dark brown eyes and was simply beautiful.

I am sure my Catholic background has contributed to my perception of how she appeared. Until the day Cyd suggested I ask about Mary's identity, there was no question in my mind as to who Mary was. At that particular time, I was satisfied with the answer.

As far as the "Book of Changes" goes, again, I was surprised by the contents of the book. A video? Really? I suppose the fact that it was a video was symbolic. Videos, like movies, are constant motion, changing images telling a story. The story is about life on earth. It's all about cycles, positive versus negative and balance. Change is energy balanced. Without it, life would cease to exist.

Perhaps I need to evaluate my own life and make the necessary changes to be balanced.

Book of Forgiveness
March 1, 2007

After having much sciatic discomfort, I went to visit Mary to ask for some kind of help. I met her on the path of "Memory Lane" (Memory Lane is explained later in the book). She said, "Walk and the pain will disappear." She was trying to help me remember what it was like to be pain-free and how happy and light it felt. I remembered how wonderful it felt to walk at Stanley Park on the nature trail on a beautiful fall day when I would stop and smell the air. It was filled with the scent of pine. I would use all my senses to enjoy everything around me. I could hear the nearby river as the water rolled over the rocks on its banks, the low drone of insects in the tall grass of the meadow and felt the warm sun on my face. It was as if my body was not there and only my consciousness was observing. Total freedom.

She made me understand that happiness and freedom were linked to lack of burden. The burden had been my anger towards the janitor of the school who had used fertilizer instead of salt for deicing on the steps. In fact, the steps were not even wet! I was the first person to use the stairs. It was like slipping on little marbles falling flat on my back against the edge of each step. The impact sent a fiery jolt straight to my head. I laid there for a moment, stunned. I knew something had to have been damaged besides my pride. I managed to get up and warned the other people to be careful. I thought, how stupid this janitor was and the anger I felt towards him because of the damage it may have caused. I have been holding onto the anger, the blame and it is stuck in my back now causing increasing physical pain.

I then thought of Bubba. I had a strange memory experience of Bubba this weekend. Bubba was one of Joe's slow students who tragically died before he could graduate from high school. I had never met him but certainly heard enough about him. As Joe said, "I will never forget Bubba." Joe had a big soft spot for him.

Anyway, I wondered why his memory arose. I was driving to Northampton and I kept thinking about him. All of a sudden, I saw a huge banner next to someone's house that said, "Welcome Home Bubba." I gasped when I saw the banner. "Wow, how weird is that?" I thought. This experience helped me make a connection. People thought Bubba was not too bright and they would lose patience with him and perhaps even got angry with him. It was not his fault.

It was not the janitor's fault using fertilizer as a deicer as I'm sure he had good intentions to keep the steps free of ice. He just made a big mistake. Unfortunately, I suffered the consequences.

I then asked Mary how do I begin forgiveness. We were suddenly next to the books in the Library and I focused on a maroon colored book. When I was about to open it, it seemed like the wind took the pages and turned them rapidly. I quickly stopped the pages from turning. The page was blank on the left. The page on the right said, "Let go." I let go of the page and the wind blew the rest of the pages.

In order for me to forgive, I have to let go, and just like the wind, the anger will be blown away and the same feeling of freedom and happiness will return just as it did on the path on "Memory Lane." Mary said I will still have discomfort from my physical injury but the karma from the anger will be gone and healing can begin.

Isn't it easy to blame someone else for our misfortunes in life? I think we tend to not look at the entire picture. What happens when we blame another person? What do we feel towards them? Probably anger for starters. We look around to see who is at fault. It seems hard to imagine that we might be part of the problem. Certainly, there has to be someone else to blame! There goes the anger, frustration and even denial. It may have been someone's mistake that caused my pain, or was it? In my situation, I could have been more careful.

It was easier to blame the janitor and it sort of felt good at the time to express my anger. The problem is, the emotion of anger is extremely strong, and it will impact our energy in a very negative way. It also lingers for quite some time.

I am sure that holding onto the anger depleted my energy and weakened my physical body so much that I eventually needed surgery for a ruptured disc. The lesson was learned the hard way.

Forgiving is not showing weakness, it takes strength and courage to forgive others. Forgiving yourself can be even harder. I believe that you can learn from an experience even if it is a negative one. So, in other words, if you can find something positive from a negative experience, then you have found balance, which then neutralizes the negative energy, anger in this case. The result will be positive. I just have to remember, I am human. I need to learn to not be so hard on myself.

You have probably heard someone say, "Just let it go." It is easier said than done. A while back I began to realize that I was holding onto "stuff." I thought about unburdening myself and tried to think of a way to unload some of the "stuff." So, I used my imagination. I thought to myself, "What does a burden look like?" Well, the first thing I saw in my mind was the proverbial black ball and chain. I began to see each link in the chain as an individual burden that needed to be released. As I observed the links in my mind, I saw each one of them turn white and disintegrate. Then I was left with the ball. I imagined filling the ball with helium and allowed it to float high in the clouds. The ball then burst and its pieces became white and disintegrated turning into rain. To my amazement, I felt so much better. It was a symbolic release. I let it go.

The Black Book
December 5, 2007

I found Mary this morning in the room with the books. She knew I had many worries and concerns in my life. She quickly showed me the books, told me to focus and I saw a black book. I removed it from the shelf and sat down to look at it. The cover had no words but had an iridescent appearance. She said, "Open it." One page seemed to have a storybook, childlike picture of a house. The opposite page had a hole in the center through which I could see the picture on the following page. The next picture was the same one except for a change in it. A little dog had been repositioned and again the following page had a hole in the middle. The next picture was also a little different. I did not understand any of this.

She said, "This book represents both present and future as viewed from a child's perspective. The present is the picture of the house, and the hole represents a view of the future. Just as in the 'Book of Truth,' the hole represents the knowing. The truth is that the future will bring change."

The message is that I can't worry about the future, as certainly change will happen. I cannot control it. Therefore, worry will change nothing. Just accept what is truly known in the present.

I believe we need to simplify our thoughts and try to take things more at face value, as do children. Just as Mary had once said to me, "Simplicity leads to completeness." Did you ever notice just how simple a child's drawing really is? They don't tend to draw all the details like clapboards on a house. Just the basics are shown. I remember when my twin grandsons were in first grade and the teacher asked the class to draw the members of their family. The boys included us in their family pictures. It was a simple drawing but it meant the world to me. We did not even live in the same house, but our close relationship was demonstrated in a simple picture.

Young children live in the moment. It is adults who are always looking forward and not enjoying what they have right now. We can always hope in the future that everything to come is good, but we anticipate too much only to get disappointed at times. Our experiences in life tend to make us more hesitant and worried. We all need to stop guessing the future. It only causes concerns or worry. You can't worry about something you can't control. Control is the operative word. However, you need to use common sense and be prepared for the future. Be aware but enjoy living.

If children worry, it is because they have learned that from us. I think it is our responsibility to teach our kids to enjoy the present and embrace the future. As parents we need to remember, they learn from example.

A Tale of Stories
January 4, 2011

I visited Mary today as I finally decided to continue with writing my book. I had stopped for a while as I found it to be too daunting a task due to my overwhelming lack of confidence.

After my initial deep breath, my visit happened within several seconds and I was in My Place. For some reason, it took a little longer than usual and I felt a little deeper in hypnosis today.

In my mind, I stood in the main room, the Library. There was a degree of clarity I had not experienced before. The French doors were wide open and the sun was shining on the books on the shelves. I could not determine if it was early morning sun or late afternoon. There was a hint of honeysuckle in the air. The room was silent. I was aware of listening to my own movements, footsteps and the swishing sound of my clothing. I realized I had never experienced this before. The books on the shelves were so distinctly clear and begging to be touched. As I softly touched them, I could feel the quality of their covers and sense their smell.

I saw a red book and took it off the shelf. Behind me was a soft brown leather chair that I had never noticed before facing the books. As I sat, I was aware of the sound of the leather rustling under my weight. A small table was next to the chair upon which a glass of lemon water was waiting for me. Comfort and peace seemed to fill the environment. I felt a strange sort of familiarity as though I had done this many times before. I continued to place my attention on the red book in my lap. The face of the book had a wide fancy gold border. The title said, "A Tale of Stories." I thought, "How strange and redundant!"

Then Mary entered the room and sat to my left in a similar chair. I greeted her with a question. "What does this mean? Why are things so clear?" She said, "This place and all the books are created from imagination." I remembered that imagination is thought, thought is energy and energy creates matter, consequently becoming reality.

I opened the book to see words on the top of the pages which said, "Notes and Journals". Below were words too small to see. I remembered viewing a book that looked like this one once before. Only those same pages were blank at the time. Could this be the same book?

As I previously stated in the entry, "Book of Many Lives", this red book looked familiar. Perhaps this is the same book I am currently writing.

I believe this red book is my story and it is told with the use of journals, parts of which function somewhat like allegories. In essence, I am telling a story of how I get answers to my own questions. The answers come as stories with a lesson and contain post session insights.

I remember asking myself, "Are these allegories simply my brain creating scenarios allowing me to reach into my subconscious soul wisdom to help me understand a conscious concern of mine? Or, are these true spiritual messages that I receive from another realm in this deep hypnotic state?" This all seemed a little confusing and scary the more I thought about it.

Mary then reminded me that when I am in My Place, I feel no fear, just peace. Fear limits the imagination. Humans, by nature, fear the unknown. It is a cause of great stress. Worry and fear do not allow time for thought.

I asked Mary how I could combat fear in my everyday life and she simply said, "Live in the present and do not worry about the next moment, as that too will become the past. When you are relaxed you can think more clearly. Use your energy wisely. Don't waste it on worry. Remember, trust is the opposite of fear."

I always looked forward to each time I experienced self-hypnosis. I never knew what to expect as I explored all sorts of wonderful places in my mind. Sometimes it seemed very confusing and difficult to understand the messages or answers I received during the sessions. Thank goodness I had Mary. At this point on my journey, however, I still questioned if she was just a figment of my imagination. I thought it would be fascinating to entertain the idea that she was a true spirit guide.

Book of Success
May 2, 2014

As I was typing some pages for the book, I suddenly felt the need to go to My Place. I spoke to Mary about my book as I was looking for some encouragement. I thought I was done with my visit and opened my eyes for just a second to realize I was not finished with my session with Mary. As I closed my eyes again, I was in the Library. She reached into the bookcase and handed me a deep maroon colored book with gold edged pages. I focused on the cover and it said, "Book of Success." Upon opening the book, I realized the individual pages were invisible and all I could see were many words superimposed on each other. It was impossible to read. I asked Mary what that meant. For the first time, she told me to figure it out myself.

I felt hot all over as I became overwhelmed with the idea that I had to do this one alone. I felt some anxiety as my poor left-brain was really struggling to make sense of this strange book.

I remembered to focus. As I did, somehow, I managed to push away all the superimposed words to get to the first words written on the first page. Now it somehow made sense to me. To be successful in something, I needed to focus. I needed to think about my goal. At that point, my goal was to be able to see the first words.

Aiming for success can feel overwhelming, setting me up for anxiety. I was so anxious that I felt hot all over. I felt frustrated that I had to depend on myself to figure out this puzzle. Success can be gauged many ways such as fame or fortune, but I think success is achieved in the little things that we do every day. Of course, not everything we do will be successful. We are human.

I never got to read the words on that first page, which was not important, but I was pleased and relieved that I figured out on my own what this lesson was about in the "Book of Success." Having a goal and focus relieves the stress and tension from a task, which then, in turn, allows me to think more clearly. Relaxation is one key to success.

How do people measure success? What really is

considered success? Is it the big things in life like graduations, high power jobs? I think success is overrated. As I stated above, it is the little things that count. The small feats of success lead up to the bigger things. Just like a marriage, it is the culmination of everyday growth together as a couple that dictates a successful marriage. Some people may stay together for years and years but is it a successful marriage if they don't get along?

    The fact that Mary left me to figure out this book shows that she wanted me to succeed by thinking for myself. Maybe she is starting to let me go on my own like a good parent teaching a child. She no longer needs to hold my hand and explain everything. Just knowing that she is still there is comforting.

    These books I have come across in the Library are just a few that were pertinent to me at the time when I needed them. I can only imagine what other books remain to be seen. The books are really just symbolic for all the knowledge of the Universe. I also believe Universal Knowledge is found in all living organisms and imprinted in our souls. We are part of that knowledge because we are part of this expanding Universe.

Chapter 10

The Gallery

I have always enjoyed art museums and visited many in my life. However, none of them can compare with the Gallery in my mind. Thinking about its vastness alone still takes my breath away. This place holds many treasures yet to be completed by the modern master artists. I was not able to focus clearly enough to view these masterpieces. I have many lessons to learn and some have come from the Gallery. The following is one of the first entries I made concerning the books in the Library and my eventual connection to the gallery.

Secrets of the Heart
January 20, 1999

I asked Mary if there was anything that she wanted to show me today. She brought me to the wall of books and told me to focus. One particular book came into view. Mary has always reminded me to focus. It seems to be extremely important to help reach a higher level of awareness. Anyway, I reached for the book. The cover was a deep purple and the title read, "Secrets of the Heart." Mary told me to just keep it close to me; however, it was not the time to open it. This certainly was intriguing, but I still followed her directions.

Secrets of the Heart II
January 15, 2000

A significant amount of time passed before the book resurfaced. I have been an artist since childhood working with different mediums. At the time, pastel was my favorite. However, I was in a bit of a slump not having created anything for a few years and I was feeling unsure if I still had it in me. The following is a description of the purple book and the Gallery.

Today I visited My Place to ask Mary if she thought I could paint again as I used to. To my surprise, she again showed me the book, "Secrets of the Heart." She said I could now open it. Each book is unique and I never know what I am going to find when I open them. Interestingly, the names of each book are very straightforward. It's the content that can be very confusing to me. I sat down on the comfortable settee that faced the open fireplace in the Library. It always has a flame that she tells me represents all the love in the world and it never dies out. There was a lovely Tiffany lamp on a small table to my right side.

As I cautiously opened the book, I thought it strange that the first page showed only a simple, large, amorphous shaped red blotch. The next page had a similar orange spot and all the other pages followed the colors of the rainbow. I said, "I don't get it!" She reminded me that each color is represented in the Chakras.

Mary then began to explain that the colors also represent the herbal plants used in medicine. She said the color of the flower, root, leaf or tincture made from the plant would match the color of the Chakra governing the organs in need of healing.

Just as she finished explaining the colors, I suddenly found myself standing in front of a heavy looking old door. I felt I should open it thinking there was a room beyond this barrier. However, much to my surprise it was a very narrow closet with several empty shelves.

Upon examining the shelves closer, I discovered a large key. It reminded me of an old-fashioned skeleton key. I held it in my hand. I could feel the weight of the rough metal. I could even smell it.

Then my attention was drawn to my right where I noticed another door similar to the closet door. This one had an oval shaped handle made of the same material as the key. I then placed the key in the lock of the door and carefully opened it.

The first thing I noticed was a clean, shiny, hardwood floor. As my eyes followed the floor, I realized there was no delineation between the floor and the walls. It gently curved up to a wall much like the shape of the bottom of a ship. There was a strange object in the middle of the floor, which appeared to be a rectangle with swirling colors. Then even stranger, in the middle of the room, I saw what looked like a small laboratory. There were empty glass cabinets above a *black counter and sink. It definitely looked out of place. Mary told me that the laboratory is symbolic of art experiments. Upon examining the laboratory, I discovered a book stored under the shelf. All artistic experiments in the different mediums were recorded in this book, the failures, and successes. Not everything produced is a masterpiece.*

I turned my attention to the walls that revealed framed paintings, one after another, like a Gallery. I tried to focus on them but they remained obscure and blurry. I followed the line of paintings as they stretched so far along the walls it seemed like I was looking down a train track as it disappeared into the horizon. I believe it symbolizes infinite subjects of inspiration. Art will continue forever.

When I looked up to see the light source, I was astonished to see there was no ceiling. Instead, I was gazing into the night sky. A million stars provided the light. I could only imagine the great masters who too looked at the very same stars. To me, all this symbolized limitless, artistic, creations spanning throughout the Universe.

Then in an instant, I was back in the room with the fireplace sitting on the settee holding the key. Mary turned to the back of the purple book, opened the pages and revealed a place for the key. I put the key in the book and closed it. The key has unlocked a secret of my heart, art.

I learned that I need to stop limiting myself due to a lack of self-esteem and lack of confidence in myself as an artist. Anything is possible with faith and focus. By creating art, I am fulfilling a debt for having been given the wonderful gift of artistic talent. I'd better get to work!

I was in awe of this amazing Gallery. It felt timeless and limitless. My questions were answered. I was putting the limits on myself.

The Second Time in The Gallery
February 24, 2000

As mentioned before in an earlier chapter, "Of Course!", Cyd recorded some sessions. The next two are unedited transcripts.

Jan closed her eyes and went deeply into her place.
"I always see my feet on a dark path in the woods. I feel the crunching under my feet, smell the dampness of the moss, and hear the wind in the trees. Animals are coming. Wow! This is different. Bear is letting me pet the top of his head. (Pause) Somebody is calling me to the house. (Pause) This is different too. (Pause) Don't see anyone there. Steps are plain wood, five steps." *(Heaves a sigh)*

"I'm in the room (Head moves) Mary says it's an unexpected visit. (Smile) She notices I have company. She says it's a pleasure to meet you. I'm introducing you to her. She seems to be excited. She says I can always sit on the couch. I'm asking her if I can visit the Gallery again. She said I could go there anytime I want. The whole thing is mine for the asking. I have so much to learn from that room. I'm supposed to go there. That's why I've got the key. (Long pause) I've got the book; there's the key; there's the doorknob."

"Wow! Strange! I step down two granite steps. I didn't see them before. I never walked here before. It echoes. There are paintings of the great masters. They are the paintings that were never painted. O-o-oh! It's strange, almost like I'm in a

Gallery of paintings that are yet to be--lost ideas--future paintings--of great masters that are yet to be. I want to know why I'm seeing these. (Sighs, turns head to right) These are paintings that should have been painted but never were Hm-m-m! But, why am I seeing them? What am I supposed to do? Paint them? I don't think so. I need to ask her. (Long pause) Hm-m-m! Huh! She says I've got a lot of work to do. I have to study the undone paintings. I have much work to do. They're lessons to me. (Pause) One door at a time. (Faint smile and pause) She is happy to see you with me because she knows you're going to help me. Am I any good? (Pause) Hm-m-m! She says I am whatever I want to be. (Pause, turns head to right) She says I'm learning how to feel and I just have to put that on paper." (Long pause, head rolls, sighs)

"I should probably go now. I have to say goodbye to my friends out there in the woods. Why have I been given this first hand to---? Hm-m-m! (Smiles, shakes head) Okay, I guess that's stronger language. I have to pick up where they left off. They're not coming back so I have to do it. Okay! (Rolls head, sighs) (Pause) (Eyes slowly open) Whew! Wow! That was weird!"

Lessons in The Gallery
March 2, 2000

Jan closes her eyes. After 45 seconds, she lifts her head. Five seconds later, she takes a deep breath. Twenty-seconds after that, she's there. (Total of 70 seconds to get to her place)

"Every time I come here it's different. Now there's a stream of water nearby--on the rocks. I can hear it (Pause) I wish my friend would walk with me again. (Pause) She's with me. (Pause) She is my friend. (Pauses, nods head) Okay. She says she can't come with me all the way--just to the steps. They're the same ones. (Shakes head) There is no railing." (Swallows).

"I'm asking Mary if I can go into that room. She hands me the book with the key. Hm-m-m! Key is cold at first--then it warms up."

"Hm-m-m! The door is a very heavy door--it's made of mahogany or something with panels in it. I unlock the door. (Pause) Someone's waiting for me in the room. I see an easel set up. (Smiles) My first lesson. (Chuckles) I'm nervous. Just look and I shall see it? Kind of do that now. Should be clearer, though, now. I've learned to see detail. I've been learning to focus. (Pause) They put their hand on mine. Hm-m-m! A piece of charcoal. I don't use charcoal, usually. They said I must use charcoal. I have to change some of my habits. Go to this first painting--requires charcoal. I don't get the message. Oh! The Masters used charcoal. I don't like using it. It's messy. I guess I have no choice." (Pause)

"I want to see who it is that's with me. I can't see who it is. Just know his hand is on mine. He's helping me draw. I tell him I can draw. He says, 'Not like this.' (Smiles) Okay! (Face changes, head moves, pause) He tells me I must have patience. Patience must be part of the first lesson. I will see more clearly if I just allow it to come. I don't know what it means, but he says because I have the heart for it. I don't understand."

"I feel the energy of the canvas. It's three-dimensional. I have to step into the painting. Got it! I got it! I've been doing that all along. Paint is like a sculpture-3-D. I almost forgot. (Pause, smiles) That's the end of the lesson today. He was reminding me. I almost forgot. (Pause) I put the key back.

Okay. I think I understand now. Okay, it's time for me to leave."

Jan comes back, opens her eyes. "Huh! Whoa! I made one heck of a connection. Once again, I can't feel my hands. I feel like I'm looking at disembodied hands."

I find it interesting that each time upon entering the Gallery, I could not see a figure of a person. I was only aware of his presence and what I heard him say.

These two sessions reminded me to feel the energy of a painting. Being an artist, I could sense the energy of the subject I planned to paint. Sometimes I would even feel my fingertips tingle as I looked at my subject. I could feel an emotion emanating from within the object or being. The more I connect with the energy, the better the painting. Every painting has a story. Stories elicit emotions. Emotions are energy, negative or positive. So, artists not only capture images, they capture the energy from within the subject. I believe that is why art is so important. It stimulates the senses and resonates within our inner core energy. Whenever I have had the opportunity to stand in front of one of the great master's paintings such as, Monet or Van Gogh, I observe the brush strokes and begin to imagine what the artist was feeling at that moment. I absorb the residual energy, which, in turn, connects me to that painting.

People often will say, "There is something about that painting." I believe, on some subconscious level, they made the connection without fully realizing they have done so. Once I have connected to the subject, I then look at the blank canvas. In my mind, I transfer the subject onto the canvas. In a way, I sometimes feel I am just tracing what is already there.

Ego and Art
July 20, 2006

    It's been a few months since I last wrote about my journeys. A lot has happened. Mary, at one point, warned me that a medical challenge would present itself and I'm afraid it has. It has now been two days since my mom passed to the other side from pneumonia and a stroke. The course of her illness certainly was a challenge. One day she would get better then get worse. My only regret is that I wasn't with her the moment she passed.

    Today, despite my heavy heart, I visited Mary in the Gallery. Yesterday she told me that there was something in the Gallery for me but I didn't have time to visit, so there I was today. I entered the Gallery only to be greeted by a deep male voice that stated he was a "master" of art. He immediately continued to tell me all sorts of information about art that I was already aware of from my education. I did not care for his manner, as he seemed a bit arrogant. I then questioned him about claiming to be a master. If he were a master, a true master, he would not be so arrogant. He would be humble and realize there is no right or only way in art. I told him he was negative and not good so I slammed the door to the Gallery.

    Then I saw Mary and I told her I didn't understand what she meant when she said there was something waiting for me in the Gallery because I expected something positive. She said, "You just experienced your own ego." It is to remind me not to allow that to interfere with my artwork in the future. Let go and just paint.

My ego, in a way, had prevented me from progressing. I thought all my endeavors had to be great for me to be happy with myself. Not all would be, so I needed to let them go. Relax and enjoy the process. Don't worry about the outcome, if it is good, then great. I believed that if my art wasn't good enough, then it would be a negative reflection on me and then I would feel poorly about myself. I wanted to be proud of all my work. I expected nothing but perfection from myself. I wanted everyone to enjoy my work. It would bother me if someone did not like it. I tried to paint what I thought others would want, not necessarily what I would like.

Having experienced my own ego through this "master" reminded me that I needed to accept my imperfections and stop being so hard on myself.

There is that saying, "You can please some of the people all of the time. You can please all of the people some of the time, but you can't please all of the people all of the time." So, I say, "Please yourself." According to my husband, I am too self-critical. I can never be satisfied with what I accomplish. There is always something better I could have done. I am always seeking approval. Our house is never clean enough. I can never get to do my art or any other hobby until everything else is done. Well, guess what? Nothing is ever done. He says that is why I cannot relax. He is right as usual.

Chapter 11

Memory Lane

After the first several years of visiting only the Library and Gallery, apparently, Mary decided to let me explore other places. Memory Lane is a narrow dirt path alongside a small brook. The water passes quickly, splashing on rocks creating a soothing, light babbling sound. There is a tree that seems to have been there forever separating the path from the brook. A short distance ahead is a thick forest where the path then forks in different directions.

This is a marvelous place to visit as it is full of surprises. It is a very different way for me to find answers to my questions. Instead of books, Mary will simply say, "You must remember." She then taps my forehead three times and I begin to feel myself go deeper into hypnosis where I then reach into my soul's memory bank.

After a moment or two, I am able to sense being in a different time and place. Sometimes I am even a different gender. Then suddenly a scene begins to develop that is unfamiliar. As the scene evolves, I find that I am part of a story. The story then unfolds and reveals the answer to my original questions. Mary, however, will further explain the story and how it relates to the questions. The following journal entries are good examples of such experiences.

Power of Love and Change
April 29, 2005

I found Mary today, only this time she took my hand and began to walk with me down Memory Lane, a new experience for me. She told me I was to remember something important, as today, whether I am aware of it or not, I needed to be strong for someone else. They will come to me and expect comfort. I presume a Reiki client. Could be anyone. Anyway, what I was supposed to "remember" was in a past life. She touched my forehead three times and said, "On the count of three you will remember." I could feel myself drifting deeper into a sea of lost memories.

I began to see water in front of me and saw that I was on a boat in the ocean. Off in the distance was an island. It seemed the boat was lost. Then suddenly I, as a man with other men, stepped onto the wet sand of a tropical beach. We walked into a small village. At first, the native people were afraid. We exchanged some things. Apparently, we remained there quite a long time, long enough for me to find a true love. The other men decided to leave and try to find the homeland again. They left and I chose to stay which demonstrated to me how strong my love was for my new life partner. My love was more powerful than fear, fear of being left behind never to see home again. I made a choice and accepted my destiny. My love *gave me strength.*

I used to think that because losing loved ones was so painful that love was a weakness, and I often wished I didn't feel it so deeply. Now I realize love is a strength to help us accept change, which happens every day. Without love we are weak. Love helps us continue on in life and overcome fear.

Mary then showed me a tulip along Memory Lane, how it blooms and eventually withers, a reminder of seasons passing only to begin again. The tulip may have a short life but we look forward to another tulip taking its place the next time spring comes. Such is life. It is accepting change with the strength of love that keeps hope for the future.

Self-Doubt and The Medicine Woman
December 2, 2005

I feel good today about myself. I realize that I can access information quickly, but, when I saw Mary this morning on Memory Lane, she seemed dark and she squeezed my hand hard. Self-doubt is shrouding the light of her face. She said it was as though I was looking into a mirror. So, I began wiping the "mirror" to see more clearly. Doubt is starting to fade.

She wanted me to remember, from a previous life, when I was initiated by a tribal medicine woman to be her successor. Mary tapped my forehead three times and I began to regress to see tall grass, dirt, and huts built on high poles and many small and larger fire pits. I was a young girl and chosen by the medicine woman as she saw my abilities to heal even though I was a child.

I remembered sitting in a cave with others and a fire pit. They put leaves of some sort on the fire. The smoke was *sickening and probably hallucinogenic to some degree. I saw spirits and then there was this thick liquid in a bowl. It was mixed with ashes and they painted some kind of design on my face. It seemed to burn. I stayed in the cave a couple of days. I am not sure what happened there but I emerged changed with a new name and the ability to heal the sick.*

In the beginning of this journal entry I thought I was feeling pretty good about these sessions and understanding that they are a gift. However, Mary was more aware than I that I had not fully accepted the gift, as there were some areas of doubt left in my mind.

In this journal I also described a tribal ceremony of some kind that was life changing. I believe I experienced the ceremonial transformation of becoming a medicine woman.

Many years ago, my husband, Joe, did a past life regression on me that I will never forget. The following is a description of my hypnosis experience as the medicine woman. I wondered if these two experiences were related somehow. By showing me this, could Mary be confirming my suspicions? Here is the amazing story.

The regression began with hearing drum sounds in the distance. I smelled smoke and heard moans and crying. As I looked around I could see grass huts on fire and complete devastation.

Joe asked me to look at my arm, a way of determining age, sex and race. When I looked at my arm I noticed how dark and old it looked. I realized in that moment that I was the medicine woman of some sort of tribe. Joe then asked me what tribe it was and I responded, "Chewa." He then asked me what my name was and I told him that it was sacred, only spoken within the tribe. My birth name was changed never to be spoken again as though, I, as a young girl, had died. He also asked me what year it was and I was unable to tell him, as time had no meaning for me.

According to the story I told, the old medicine woman had warned the tribe of an impending attack by another tribe. Those who believed the medicine woman took cover in a cave. Those who stayed behind suffered the consequences. That was the end of the regression.

At the time of that regression, I just thought it was interesting but never pursued any of the information. Several years later when I was looking up a word in the dictionary, (yes, a real dictionary) I saw the word, "Chewa." I was stunned. I then Googled it and found that the Chewa people originated from Zaire and immigrated to northern Zambia, then to central Malawi where they still live. I also discovered there is a Chewa Mask. The mask has scarifications that depict a respected woman who has undergone initiation. Chewa women can also become chiefs. I found the similarity between both regressions quite interesting.

Reading Energy
March 4, 2011

The following journal entry speaks about the Akashic Records and the soul consciousness, which I spoke about in a previous chapter, "The Library".

I visited Mary today. I have begun writing my book and

I did some research about the Akashic Records and found some information online. Then I decided to ask Mary about what I found.

She took me to Memory Lane and we just stood there. She pointed to the forest ahead. She said, "That is where everything is really recorded. Everything about the Universe is recorded in the energy within all of Nature. The ability to know the truth comes from the ability to read energy."

As humans, our physical bodies impede us. I asked her if she could teach me to read the energies. She told me to place my hand in the water of the stream we stood near and become one with the water and read its energy. I placed my hand in the water, and she asked me to tell her what I could read from the water. I said that all I could read was that it was cold and wet. I had trouble getting past the physical sensations. As my hand became numb, I realized that the water was drawing my energy and, in a way, asking me to join it.

I suddenly understood what she meant by me becoming one with the water. The only way I could read the energy of the water was to become part of it. Maybe that explains why people who nearly drown will say that they were feeling a gentle peacefulness just before they were saved and brought back to life. Perhaps the peacefulness was being one with the water.

Mary said, "You can read energy with your soul consciousness when unhindered by the physical. Some people are gifted with the ability to temporarily leave their bodies and, therefore, their soul consciousness is free to be at one with nature and read the energies."

The energies hold the knowledge of the Universe. The books in the Library of my mind hold all that information. Mary *has told me, I have written all these books myself over a millennium. It is my imagination and thought that has created their physical appearance so that I could easily retrieve the knowledge in my hypnotic state. This all makes sense to me now.*

The mansion and the books and all the wonderful places I visit in my mind are created by me on the soul conscious level. In other words, I believe we all carry this information in our soul. It is a matter of retrieval.

When we no longer have our bodies to house our souls, we become part of the energies around us again. We will then read the energies and record them in our soul. If only we could hold onto their secrets and remember them easily. I know sometime in the future I will return in another life and maybe further unravel the mysteries of my soul.

I believe we are all connected on the soul conscious level which is collectively the Universal Consciousness as I spoke about in the "Introduction". Perhaps humanity is not ready to accept the lessons that are imprinted on our souls. Accepting the truth about yourself is sometimes difficult. Too bad we cannot tap into our soul consciousness more easily. The wisdom would probably lead to a more peaceful world.

Past Life, Financial Insecurities
October 6, 2012

I decided to visit Mary today and delve into my lifelong issue of financial insecurities. She guided me to Memory Lane. She touched my forehead three times and asked me to go deep to a time when I could remember having no worries about anything. I saw myself as a little girl about two or three in my father's garden picking some flowers and playing in the dirt.

Then she told me to go back farther to another life. I found myself in an old inner city. I felt very young, a boy of about six or seven looking for food in the garbage behind a building. There were several other children there as well. Then suddenly, a man threw open a door in the alley. He was large with a white apron. All the children, including myself, dropped everything and ran in all directions like a pack of rats. However, he caught one child and brought him into the building. We all knew this was bad. We knew if we were caught, we were doomed and were sent to an orphanage, where life would be a living hell. It was much better to live in the streets. At least you were free.

To get larger clothes, we would steal from clotheslines, always watching out so not to be caught. The children knew each other and they were family. Apparently, my mother died in childbirth and my father was put in jail because he owed taxes. Somehow, I escaped to freedom. I managed to grow up and get a job as a Newsy. I became a reporter because I was so street smart and grew to be a fine adult but never got over the financial insecurities.

The point of the story is that I still hold onto those fears even though I have never experienced that extreme loneliness, poverty or loss in my present life. My soul needs to let go of this. That is one reason why I am here, to rid my soul of this burden and others. Next question. How?

This experience was surprisingly very emotional for me. That young boy had very little he could call his own. Yet, somehow, he survived on the streets and grew up all the wiser. The lessons he learned at such a young age gave him the strength he needed to succeed for the rest of his life.

I can only imagine the terror, anger, and frustration. He learned to steal to survive and had also been stolen from. It was a hard life. Yet, at the same time, he found a sense of family among the other children. He learned responsibility for himself and others. He learned compassion and love. Yet, the memory of the struggles and insecurities still haunted him.

During a past life regression, the emotions felt are very raw and real. I can sense the individual's personality and feel as though I was looking through their eyes. When I return to my normal consciousness, I still remember what transpired during the regression with great detail including the emotions.

These sessions all remind me how important and precious every moment is in this life. Appreciation for what you have is the first step to happiness and security. Memory Lane's natural surroundings create a sense of peace, a peace I try to remember each day.

Chapter 12

The Classroom

The Classroom is situated next to the Library. I have frequented this room many more times than I have recorded. It is the place where I find the most comfort. I describe it in great detail in the journal entry below.

The Classroom
May 4, 2006

  As I arrived at My Place to visit Mary, I suddenly found myself standing in front of a very old looking heavy door. I opened it and stepped into a room that was devoid of people. It seemed dark despite the light that came from a massive window stretching clear across the room looking out onto a beautiful nature scene of rolling meadows and forest.
  I noticed there were pews, like in a church, facing the window. On the left, there was an empty stage and, on the right, a huge clock with a pendulum. It reminded me of the large clock in the story of "Alice in Wonderland." I sat down in

the front row of the pews. Then Mary sat down to the right of me. She said, "This is the Classroom."

"The stage on the left represents everyday life on earth for people who are the actors. The clock is on the opposite wall so the actors can watch the time and know when to play their part. The pews facing the window are for those who show more interest in learning in this life." I asked where the teacher was and she said, "You are looking at it, Nature." She said it is time for me to explore more of My Place which is part of another plane of existence. I can still visit the other places if I wish. I think this experience is showing me that I prefer not to go through life as an actor but rather a student and study. I certainly have a lot to learn.

The Classroom has become by far one of my favorite places to visit with Mary. It is quiet like a church lending to contemplation and peacefulness and where I often start to visit Mary only to find myself going somewhere else as demonstrated in the journal below.

The Studio
February 7, 2007

I met Mary in the Classroom this morning. I had questions to ask her about the direction I was going in my life. I talked. She listened. Then I found myself drifting in thought to creating a design for jewelry. I guess I was not very focused.

Mary then spoke of the Book of Creativity but did not show it to me. Instead, she said there was another room to see, a studio. I took her hand and I saw an old large building with windows from floor to ceiling. Inside the studio, I was *aware of a messy looking sink and some covered easels. I said it looked familiar. I had seen it in a past life regression I experienced once before.*

I looked out the window and there appeared to be a city. For a moment I lost my focus again. Then my thoughts turned to a countryside view much like Norman Rockwell's studio in the Berkshires. I had that vision in my head when I realized I was still sitting in the Classroom with Mary. I had difficulty maintaining my focus today. I noticed the drifting thoughts did not seem as real as the classroom, Library, or the Gallery. I asked Mary why I could not concentrate. She said it was because I lack incentive and true desire. I guess I have to work on that.

I believe she did not show me the Book of Creativity because I was not ready to see it. I needed true desire and incentive to appreciate such a book. The studio reminded me of the one I experienced through a past life regression many years before.

In that regression, I envisioned a large room with a tall ceiling and long windows. Leaning along the wall were many covered canvases. The room was sparse of furniture except for a few easels randomly positioned. The view from the window was that of a cobblestone street. Somehow, I knew it was in France.

I saw "myself" as a middle-aged man, slight of build, placing paintings in a horse drawn cart. In that moment I knew this man was the artist who had no family and lived for his art. He seemed lonely but surviving for the love of his art. At the time of this regression, I thought it was interesting but never saw any meaning that I could relate to in my current life.

Now, after re-experiencing the studio, I see the stark difference between the man in France and me in this lifetime. I think I am spread too thin with being busy. Raising a family, running a business, school etc. has certainly taken a great deal of time and effort. Then I have to ask myself if that is just an excuse. Other people have managed to be successful with their art and handled life as well. What is my true desire? Why do I lack incentive?

I hoped I could find some answers to these questions and many others in the classroom.

Knowing and Hope
December 6, 2008

It has been a while since I journaled. I certainly have visited Mary quite a bit since my last entry but failed to write it down. Since my memory is not as good anymore, I'd better write this ASAP. I have been preoccupied with my sister's cancer and things have been looking grim. She was told she was probably Stage 4. I reached a point last night when my fear of losing her completely overwhelmed me. Today, I can't stop the tears. Since I always find some solace in my journeys, I figured today would be a good time to visit Mary.

Mary was in the Classroom and I was looking out the window at a winter scene that was strikingly beautiful. Each season has a purpose to it even when things appear to be frozen and lifeless as in winter. Life is just taking a break and resting, waiting for the right time to regenerate again. It is time to reflect and plan ahead as there will always be a new season to perhaps do things better than the last one.

Maybe that is what illness does for us. It forces us to

take a break so we can make better plans for the future. Anyway, Mary assures me Marie is going to be all right. She makes me feel it is true. She tells me, "Knowing creates peace." When we have passed to the other side, we gain wisdom or knowing that we wished we had when we were in physical form and especially in our youth. Maybe we would have done things differently or enjoyed our life more.

Imagine if we were already born with all the wisdom and knowledge there would be no purpose to experiencing life. We would probably not make mistakes or even have an excuse for our mistakes like, "I'm only human."

Perhaps humor would not be the same either, if it existed at all. Doesn't humor come from human error and idiosyncrasies? I'm sure everything would be more peaceful with wisdom and knowledge. No need to deal with stress. There wouldn't be any. We would just simply say, "I accept this", and let it go because we knew what the outcome was going to be. There would be no exploration of any kind. In my opinion, knowing everything could be quite boring.

I think we come to earth as humans to go on an adventure trip, not knowing what is around the next corner. Try to imagine we are all in this big movie of sorts. Souls on the other side have first row seats watching us, as we are their entertainment. Perhaps this looks so exciting to souls that they want to join in on the act so they come back as a human again.

Of course, all of this is said with tongue in cheek. My point is, life is an adventure into the unknown searching for knowledge. It is the manner in which we gain that knowledge that enhances our spiritual evolution. Hope is that the knowledge we gain improves our lives as individuals as well as that of humankind.

By the way, Mary was correct again, my sister was all right! As I wrote in Chapter 4 in the story of my friend Karen and her deceased brother who said, "Your sister is going to be all right, you know", my sister, as of this writing, has been a cancer survivor for more than ten years.

**Unlocking the Door
December 21, 2013**

I found Mary in the Classroom today. She stood in front of the large window. Suddenly she was consumed with fire then turned to water. It happened so quickly I did not have time to react. Returning to her normal form, she said that my fear of fire and water is due to my distrust of them. Fire and water are opposing elements. I feel I am not in control of things.

I am always tense even when I think I am relaxed. She said once I understand and learn to trust the water and trust the fire, I will be truly relaxed. Water and fire must be symbolic of something else.

She showed me a door with a lock and key. I have begun to slowly unlock this door which I am sure has my answers. It will take many keys to unlock it. Each key turns the lock just a little.

I said that if I could make my connections and open the door, my logical left brain could relax because it would be satisfied having found some answers. She corrected me. She said it would help my emotional right brain instead, as it is the emotions of fear that create my subconscious tension. By relaxing the right brain, my left brain can then think clearly and form the correct conclusions. Exercise, diet and taking care of my body will help to allow me more longevity. It would afford me more time to help other people understand what I am learning. She said I have many gifts and I need to find them and share with others. Only then will I find peace and serve my purposes.

So, by taking care of myself better, I will have enough time to finally unlock that door in my mind which I think is blocking my abilities to create art and who knows what else. Maybe the very thing I think will be unlocked, my art, is what will unlock the door. Isn't art correlated with the right side of the brain? The door is probably just symbolic. Deep inside I already hold the keys. I just need to find and use them.

I have always had a primal fear response to fire and water. I have worked at finding a reasonable cause for such reactions. I have been past life regressed to when these phobias may have started.

During one session, the hypnotherapist said, "Go back in time when water was an issue." I found myself in several predicaments where I believe I had drowned or had near drowning experiences in different lives. However, the last experience during that session was one of not enough water and dying of thirst. I realized after the session, the therapist had said, "when water was an issue." Certainly, not having enough water could be an issue. I took her words quite literally during the hypnosis.

I have not explored the fire issue as of yet. Who knows, maybe I was burned at the stake in a past life! Mary has said in the past that I need to face my fears in order to trust again.

She has also said that fear is the opposite of trust. When you are fearful, you are certainly not feeling in control of anything.

I know that I am generally a tense person. I have to remind myself to lower my shoulders as they are always hunched up. My startle reflex is off the wall even during my hypnosis sessions. Any unusual noise and you can peel me off the ceiling. I am generally hypersensitive to outside stimuli like smelling something before everyone else does. My point is I have trouble relaxing.

Metaphorically, there is a door to be unlocked in my psyche. It figures it would take several keys to unlock my door! There can't be one simple key.

A few months later, something remarkable happened. Much to my surprise, I came upon an unexpected change in my journey.

The Blue Room
March 22, 2014

I visited Mary today. I began in the Library with much clarity as though I was really standing in the sunlight, feeling its warmth as it cascaded across the shiny parquet floors and gently reached up against the books. I saw two brown leather chairs with a small table between them. On the table was the black lacquered box that holds signs, symbols and musical notes, a gift from the past.

Mary was there dressed in a different material. It was a heavy, iridescent, brocade-like fabric. She said it was for a great celebration. I asked her, "What is the occasion?" She said, "It is a party to celebrate your remembering." She took me into a large room filled with my deceased family, friends, artists, and others. Some were dressed in old-fashioned attire from many different eras and cultures. I couldn't believe what I was seeing. Mary then removed the hooded part of her garment. That never happened before! I felt so completely overwhelmed and confused that I just needed to retreat to the Classroom to try to understand what was happening. I did not feel like I had any breakthroughs in my memory to celebrate.

Once in the quiet of the Classroom, Mary said that Elaine, my sister-in-law, was waiting for me on the patio. I was so happy to see her and she was exuberant. She seemed happy for me, almost giddy. I said that I still didn't understand what was happening. Elaine then told me that there is a room above me that is blue and I just need to walk in. She said the door is no longer locked. That is why she is so happy for me. So, all of a sudden, I was standing in front of a heavy, dark paneled door that opened with ease. The room had blue walls and one window, nothing else.

As I stood in the room, I realized that the space of the room was filling with blue light. The light became so thick that I could no longer see the walls or window. It engulfed me.

To better understand the significance of the blue room, Mary told me to read about the spiritual meaning of blue light. With that, I was back in my family room.

As directed, I went online and looked up, "Spiritual meaning of blue light." Apparently, blue is calming, spiritual and represents inspiration. Inspiration is certainly what I have been lacking as far as my art is concerned. The color blue connects us to our higher power or our soul. The more I read about blue light in several different websites, the more I realized how it describes my personality. Maybe that is what the celebration is all about, my discovering who I really am. Mary has always said, "You must remember." I suppose it is deep within me and will surface when needed.

The celebration was a surprise and especially overwhelming to see so many souls from this life as well as previous lives as I surmise. All these people seemed so happy and they were having a good time at the party. It was wonderful to see Elaine as she joined the party.

The sessions I have journaled about are very revealing of who I am, personality, faults, desires, and values. I think these experiences help me to understand myself on a very deep level. Introspection has its drawbacks, however. It points out the negatives as well as the positives. I see my weaknesses. On the other hand, I have an opportunity to work on those weaknesses as I have learned to accept them as part of who I am.

I would probably be very upset and dejected if another person pointed out my weaknesses. However, by seeing them for myself through the process of these sessions, I can handle criticism much better. Sometimes, it is very hard to accept the fact that you could be either wrong or have failed in some way. But if you can admit to yourself on a sincere level your own shortcomings, it is easier to make the necessary changes in your life to improve yourself.

Perhaps this room holds other great treasures. For now, I am satisfied with the experience and comfort of the room with the blue light.

Chapter 13

The Secret Garden

As a youngster, I had heard of the children's story, "The Secret Garden", but, honestly, I never read it. I have seen artistic perceptions of the outside appearance of the gate to the garden but that is all that is familiar to me about the book. I thought it would be interesting to find out what the story was about so I searched a website which gave a quick summary. I am amazed by how I have found this place in my mind, and by the correlation between the story and my own secret garden.

The characters in the story, "The Secret Garden", were children who had suffered psychological trauma in different ways. So, in a nutshell, the discovery of the garden helped to heal them. The garden in my mind has also been a healing place. I visit this garden quite often.

I usually find myself sitting on a white bench under a small arbor of white flowers. Mary is always seated to my left and wears a long white robe-like dress with gold trim on the edges. It is always peaceful in the garden.

Mary tells me that the snapdragon is my flower. When she first mentioned that flower, I did not understand why it would be so important to me. I could not find any spiritual connection. In fact, I had never planted it in any garden. Last year was the first time I decided to grow some in the back yard to see what was so special. As I watched it grow, I noticed that it bloomed the entire season. If I cut it, it grew even more. It also comes in different colors. I guess I never paid much attention to the snapdragon. It really is a beautiful flower. If I were to look for the symbolism, I would probably say that it represents longevity, renewal, and diversity. I do enjoy these qualities.

On the following pages, I have included only a few sessions that I thought were especially important. This session describes the first time I visited the Secret Garden.

The Secret Garden
March 14, 2007

Today I found Mary standing next to the tree on the path of Memory Lane. I asked the significance of this tree. She said, "It simply represents the path. The trunk is straight as is the beginning of the path and its branches are the forks in the path." I have to choose what direction I want to follow.

I began a short walk with her down one of the paths and I came upon what looked like a hidden garden. Its appearance reminded me of the picture on the storybook, "The Secret Garden." Before I entered the gate, Mary told me to focus carefully on every detail. I began to see a brick wall covered in vines. There were two gray granite steps covered with moss and vines that led up to a wooden door. The door was a dark, heavily weathered wood with a large wrought iron ring for a handle. As I opened the door I heard it crack and creak from its heavy weight and from probably not having been disturbed for some time.

I entered the garden stepping onto a cool brick path. I was aware of the sound of water bubbling and the fragrance of lemon and orange trees. There were beautiful roses, absolutely breathtaking.

In stark contrast, as I looked at Mary, I saw a darkness about her face. I recognized this as my fear reflected in her face. I could not possibly understand where that could be coming from since I was so happy in this place. She then pointed to the garden. The other half of the garden was dead, no life at all. I didn't know what to think. She said that this secret garden represented me. Part of me is flourishing but my fears have destroyed the other half. She told me that I must conquer my fears to bring back the garden. I must stop holding on to the fear of failure and other fears.

I put my hands in front of me facing the garden and felt the garden begin to sprout as in the springtime. I need to focus on living and flourishing. If I put my fears to rest, that space will thrive and my Secret Garden will be alive and well, all of it.

Fear really is our worst enemy along with worry. Mary has shown me this amazing garden that represents trust and peacefulness, certainly the opposite of fear and worry. She has told me that worry will be the cause of my demise unless I do something about it. The Secret Garden was a visual warning to me. I choose to grow my garden.

I remember the time I visited Mary and found her on the patio outside the mansion. As I called to her, she turned around to face me. I was horrified, as she looked dark and hideous. Then, instantly, she turned into water and I watched as the water flowed toward the ocean in the distance. Then she reappeared as her usual bright self. I asked her, "What just happened?" She said, "You have just viewed your own fear." I certainly was frightened by what I saw and now I understand how fear destroys and perpetuates more fear.

Another time during a visit with Mary, we were standing on some sand dunes. She pointed in the direction over the top of a dune. I climbed the dune and suddenly there appeared a large ball of light. The base of the light was on fire. Then from the light, I saw an outstretched hand as though it was beckoning me to take it. I chose not to out of fear. Immediately, the light disappeared and I was left alone on the dune. When I turned I saw Mary and asked her, "What *was* that?" She responded, "That was your higher self." I was not ready to trust.

Since trust is the opposite of fear, in order to overcome fear, I must first understand where the fear comes from and trust myself to face the fear. I need to develop compassion for myself. Yes, compassion. When I am feeling fearful, I feel very childlike and weak. I am vulnerable which sets me up for more fear and worry.

Fear feeds fear. Instead, I need to stand outside myself and feel compassion for my own inner child as a mother comforting her scared little one. This separation of self leads to a new perspective because I am now viewing a situation from outside with a different emotional attachment. Panic and fear would no longer have the grip on me. My logical left brain then would have a chance to make order of a situation. My emotional right brain would then calm down.

It is certainly easier said than done but remembering the goal of growth and promise of new life makes it all worth the effort. It is hard work to overcome fear. It has taken time to make my garden grow and flourish.

Seed of Life
March 26, 2011

I wanted to say hello to Mary and tell her how truly happy I am. We met in the Classroom. It was a beautiful day as I gazed through the large window of the Classroom, which overlooked rolling hills, and tree lined meadows.

I told Mary of the extreme depth of love and admiration I had for my husband. How fortunate I felt in all aspects of my life. I could feel emotions welling up and exploding with tears of joy.

I wanted to give Mary something to show my appreciation for all she has done for me. I just couldn't think of anything appropriate so I asked her what she would like. She showed me lilies. I have all kinds in my Secret Garden so I suggested we go there. Then she said, "Wait, it is time to plant the seed." I had forgotten about that seed. A while ago she gave me a round, heavy, brass ball containing the Seed of Life and she told me I would plant it when it was time.

Now, as I entered my garden, everything was flourishing. Again, I could feel the cool brick and soft moss beneath my feet. The aroma of the lilies was almost overpowering. I heard the water bubbling from the right-hand corner of the garden. We stood looking at the far end of the garden in the corner where a small portion of earth was still barren. She indicated that was a good place to plant it. I began to dig a small hole in the ground. I opened the brass ball and found a small round seed in a soft bed of moss. I placed it with the moss in the ground and lightly covered it with earth.

Suddenly I noticed my father was standing next to me. I was again overcome with emotion and I asked him to just hold me as I found myself sobbing with unbelievable happiness.

I still didn't understand what the Seed of Life really was. I just knew it was planted. I have to wait and see what grows.

Artful Insight
May 4, 2013

Today I wanted to visit my Secret Garden. As usual, I expected to see Mary there as well. However, this time she had someone else with her. I saw a man in a black suit standing next to her. The man sat down on the bench next to me. As I looked at his face, I recognized him as the man in a portrait I had painted many years ago. It is probably my best painting. I did the painting from a photo in a magazine. The man appeared to be an elderly, homeless, blind, black gentleman with gray hair and tattered clothing. I titled the portrait "Blind Distinction." His inner pride and gentleness are what I saw in his blind eyes. However, as I looked at him in my garden, he seemed healthy and definitely not blind.

I asked him his name and he replied, "Abraham, but call me Abe." He was dressed in a black suit not torn or tattered. He said, "They thought I should look nice." He thanked me for *immortalizing him in the portrait. He then knelt down on one knee. He begged me to do my artwork. I said that I was having trouble getting inspiration. He told me that everything has inspiration within it. I just need to feel it. That is the secret to finding inspiration.*

He said I was one of the best in the past, and I have the next 40 years to complete my work. (Yes, that would make me 103 years old, but that is just potential!) *Now is the time to get going on painting. I thanked him and came back to my family room.*

After this session was over, I walked to the dining room where his portrait is hung. I looked at the painting and as if he were talking to me, I began to realize something. When I paint, I am creating a physical image but what I am really painting is the very essence of the subject.

For instance, if you were to view a painting of an apple, you could take it for face value and just think it was a pretty apple. In order to see what is so special about that apple, you need to look beyond the surface of that painting. Ask yourself, "What is so special about this apple that the artist found inspiration to paint it?" Take a good look at that apple. What drew your attention to it in the first place? Was it the color that caught your attention or something else? Every painting has a story. Whatever the case may be, pieces of art are important because they remind us that what we see on the physical surface, may not be all there is to see. Abe's outward appearance in the painting could lead us to believe that he was just an old bum. Looking beyond the surface, he has a life story to be told. Capturing but a second in time on canvas can tell a lifetime of living.

Finally, you could say that Abe got through to me. It is amazing that it took the energy of the subject of my own artwork to bring back the secret of inspiration I so desperately sought. I remembered how I felt the day I began his painting. There was something in his blind eyes that attracted my attention. That is when I felt the inspiration to paint. I saw the pride inside this impoverished man as he gazed straight ahead as though he could see what was in front of him. It was as if I could sense what he was thinking. At that moment I felt an insatiable urge to paint and I kept painting until it was finished. That was true inspiration.

Chapter 14

More Lessons

There are so many lessons to learn in this life. So many questions that seem to go unanswered. I believe the life I chose to lead was meant to give me the experiences needed to further my spiritual evolvement. I also believe I was spiritually guided in that direction to best suit my needs even if I didn't realize it. Hindsight is 20/20. I guess we will find our answers after we have left this world or, earth school, as some have called it. Whatever the case may be, there is a lot to learn in so little time. The following journal entries shed light on some of my other questions.

Soul Mates
March 24, 2003

When I visited Mary today, she knew I had a question about the woman's disembodied voice I heard many years ago. It has bothered me for some time. She told me that she was a guide from long ago and I will someday hear her voice again.

I then asked about the man's voice I heard once. She said he was a soul mate from my past. She explained that we all have many soul mates, one for every aspect of ourselves, i.e. art, healing, family etc. Sometimes we meet up with the same one repeatedly in different lifetimes. We may not always marry them but could just be friends or relatives depending on what lessons are needed for that lifetime.

Soul mates share a true unconditional love. There should be no jealousy and each has a purpose that should be respected.

Having had the experience of hearing a disembodied woman clearly speak to me many years ago is very disconcerting, to say the least. It was not a voice I heard in my head. Her message was private so I won't go into details but I was completely stunned. The only other time I heard a voice speak to me was when I was by myself at the cottage on Cape Cod. It was a man's voice that said, "Tenth time, I love you." I looked everywhere but found no one. It was as if he were standing right next to me! These two experiences have left me with many questions and haunted me for many years. I guess I felt some relief from Mary's explanation.

I always thought of a soul mate as that person with whom I would spend the rest of my life. I assumed it would mean a husband. I never gave any thought to having many soul mates for other areas of my life as well.

We certainly learn from other people but not all are soul mates. Perhaps you have come across someone who shares a passion, for example, music or art to the point where they teach you and you teach them. You both reach each other on a deep soul level of understanding and appreciation. I imagine that person would also be a soul mate.

Appreciating Parents
April 2, 2003

I saw Mary again today. Her face is finally getting brighter. She is happy for me because I have realized something important. I should be pleased to have the opportunity to take my mother to the doctor amongst other things, which tends to be a chore right now. There will come a day when I no longer have her and would do anything just to be with her again. I would miss her that much.

I know it is not fun to have to wait for appointments or do an extra run to the drug store or grocery store, but life without her at all would feel awful. I wish I had my dad so I could complain about taking care of him. At least I would have him. He has been gone for so long now. No matter how many years pass, the feelings don't change.

My parents did the best they could for my sister and me. I need to remember parents are people too. They have faults and flaws. Children, no matter what the age, tend to put their parents on a pedestal. The parent is supposed to be invincible. They cannot get old. They are always supposed to be there for us. When the parents begin to age and can no longer function like they used to, we suddenly realize and may say, "You mean we now have to take care of them?" Maybe we get a little bit angry to think they are changing. Maybe we forget all the things they did for us and never complained.

So, my point is that cherishing time with them no

matter what the circumstance is important. Concentrate on the good memories of my mom now while I have her. Mary said I didn't need a book today. I'm starting to remember important things about living.

"From the cradle to the grave" is a common phrase referencing an entire lifetime. Any good parent knows that from the time their child is even conceived, their world is changed forever, and it is no longer about them. There is a new little person coming into this world. It is up to parents to care for and nurture this little stranger. The love for a child is unmatched by any other love. That child is part of you.

Children do not come with instructions so we do our best. There are times the child lets you know they have a mind of their own. When that happens, things can get interesting. Nevertheless, parents are there to support them and guide them.

Sometimes, from the child's perspective depending on the age, parents are either "cool" or "embarrassing." The child has his or her own life to live and may not want the advice or guidance that the parent is so willing to give. Even as children reach adulthood, their perception of parents is that they will always be there for them. The adult child, subconsciously, places the parent in a category aside from all others. The adult child may take their parents for granted without realizing how much they still depend upon them.

Yes, it is difficult to rearrange your busy schedule to tend to the needs of an ailing parent. It can get very frustrating if they cannot hear you as well as you think they should. Let's face it. It is not always easy to deal with the needs of older parents. However, the parents understand as they too were in your shoes with their ailing parents, your grandparents. So, the cycle continues with each generation.

I believe it is important to see your parents as people who had flaws as well as hopes and dreams just like you. It takes understanding, patience, and love to see them in a different light. To truly appreciate your parents is a gift from the soul. That appreciation deepens the love and connection you have with your parents. Don't wait until they are gone.

I have a suggestion. Sit down with your parents and tape the visit, video or audio. Ask them to tell you about their life, or what it was like growing up in their era. Look at the objects in their home that are near and dear to them. Ask them what was the story behind Aunt Edna's desk or that old vase that you can remember always sitting on the mantel. I did just that with my mom. She really got into it after a couple of minutes. It was a great opportunity to learn more about the family treasures which I had taken for granted as just objects that could so easily be discarded after she died.

At some point, my daughter had a school project that involved interviewing someone in my mother's generation to talk about what it was like growing up. I will always cherish the sound of her voice describing what it was like in the horse and buggy days. She had such delight in her voice as she relayed what it was like as a little child on "May Day" which is the first day of May. Apparently, children would gather little wild flowers and run up to a person's house, knock on the door, leave the flowers then run away as fast as they could. If they got caught, they would get a kiss.

Once in a while I listen to the CD and feel the warmth of her voice again. I never got the chance to do that with my father. All I have are photos and memories.

The Deer and the Cliff
September 30, 2007

It has been a tough spring and summer. I had surgery for my back and now I am six weeks postoperative. The pain is gone but I need to be careful. I had not visited Mary in a long time so I decided to try today.

The first thing I saw was a huge tree in front of me. Somehow it felt comforting in an odd way. I was looking for Mary but I was alone in this forest. Then I saw a deer and it sort of beckoned me to follow it so I did. It led me down a narrow path crossing a little babbling brook. Then the deer stopped at the edge of a cliff which had a spectacular view of snow-covered mountains and green valleys. The deer suddenly turned back and ran off in a hurry. I did not care as I stood there taking in the vista.

Then I had a strange sense of fear that someone, hiding in the shadows, was about to push me off the cliff. I shook off the thought and bravely looked down the side of the cliff. It was so steep I could not see the bottom. Then I noticed to my left there was a small tree with a thick rope tied to a branch. It dangled straight down but too short to be of any help getting down the cliff. At that point I just wanted to go back to the large tree I saw at the beginning of the forest. Instantly, I was there again.

Then I saw Mary and asked her what that was all about. She said the tree is my strength and safety. Following the deer was my innocent trust that it would lead me somewhere. It left me at the cliff where I saw great beauty in the distance but faced decision and fear. Even though I managed to shake the fear I chose the tree for my safety and strength, as I felt vulnerable at the cliff. She said I would come upon a situation in my life that I will recognize as the tree, the deer, and the cliff. I will remember this to help me get through a tough decision. I guess it comes down to a choice again. Do I take a risk or be safe?

Certainly, life is full of decisions or choices we have to make. Some are more difficult than others. How do we make our decisions? What determines our choices? How many factors are involved? Are our decisions based on emotions like fear or is it knowledge? I am talking about our logical left brain versus emotional right brain. Do those who function based on their left brain make better decisions? Perhaps the right-brained individual can see another side based on emotions and wisdom that would make a better determination. No matter what process is involved, a decision is made which ultimately brings about change.

The symbolism of the deer and the cliff is, I feel, straight forward. The deer is the innocence and freedom. It invokes trust, as the deer is a non-threatening creature. It reminded me of Bambi! Yet, the deer left me alone to make a choice to retreat or pursue a seemingly dangerous and impossible task. I chose to retreat. Was it an emotional choice or logical decision? Probably, it was a little of both. Maybe the day will come when I need to make a serious decision. I will have to accept my choice and move on.

Acceptance
May 27, 2008

Just three more days of this horrible back and leg pain. I am awaiting my second back surgery. I unhooked the phone because I didn't want to be disturbed. It gave me a strange sense of freedom not having to communicate with anyone for a while. I'm looking forward to surgery, as they believe it will relieve the pain, which has become, at times, intolerable. My biggest fear is that there has been too much damage done to the nerve and I will still have pain.

I decided to take advantage of my solitude and try to visit Mary again but I am tired of everything being so cryptic. I found her in the garden and I spoke of my fear. Again, she said I must trust to replace fear. I need to have more patience with myself. I stated my fear of being no better after surgery and also needing help from others.

Then, I believe, a spiritual master entered the scene. He took my hand and we sat down on a bench. He held my hand and said it is all right to accept help and I argued that what makes me happy is doing things for other people. Maybe that is selfish because I get such pleasure from helping others. He said that I needed to learn to accept help. He made a cross sign on my forehead. I asked that I continue to be capable of doing what makes me happy. He told me I didn't understand. He was right, I didn't. I needed to learn about humility.

Mary then said she had something to give me. We walked to a rose bush. She handed me a rose without thorns. It represented sweetness, peace, newness, and softness. She said to hold it close to my heart as a reminder that there is and must be balance. In other words, what you put out must come back and you must accept the return in order to have balance in your life. Only then can you be truly happy.

So, I can give all I want and perhaps it is selfish, but to balance it, accepting it back is humbling. I guess then that the opposite of selfishness is humility. The opposite of fear is trust. Two more lessons I have to learn.

    Finally, relief from the ruptured disc for the second time! The second time was definitely harder to recover as so much damage and scarring had occurred from the first surgery. Fear is difficult to overcome when you are faced with uncontrollable pain whether it is physical or emotional. Fear is a primal response meant to get the adrenalin flowing for fight or flight. However, when the fear is so overwhelming that you are frozen in place, you have a big problem! I believe that a mild fear or concern can turn into a much larger anxiety if we dwell on that fear and not let it go. As my husband so wisely states, "There is no use in worrying about something you cannot do anything about." I have to remind myself of that quote.

    Mary tells me that trust will take away fear. If you can learn to trust that everything works out in the end, it can alleviate some of the fears. It is always that unknown. I tried to project my thoughts beyond the day of surgery to a point where I was pain-free. In my mind, I looked back on the day of surgery with no emotion as it was in the past. It was over. The surgery was successful and free of fears. I trusted that day would come and it did.

    I wanted to get back to my life of helping others as it made me feel happy. To accept help, on the other hand, is very difficult for me. In fact, I don't know how to accept a compliment without feeling a little embarrassed. I must remind myself of the need for balance. You can give all you want but if you cannot accept anything in return, your life will be out of balance. On some level, your energy vibration could suffer. Those who wish to give to you will feel that you do not value their help and, therefore, perpetuate their imbalance.

Opening Doors
March 1, 2009

I began to feel sad thinking of the past and went to find Mary. She showed me the key again in the "Secrets of The Heart" book. I took it out of the book and placed it over my heart. Immediately, it just disappeared into my heart. She said I could use it anytime to open any door in my mind.

Suddenly I was in this long hallway with several doors. So, I tried it on a door that was to my right. I opened it and saw a darkened room with one dull lamp on in the corner. I recognized my grandfather's old, gray, leather chair. I sat in it and it felt familiar and comfortable. Then I felt like I was thrust backward in time with so many thoughts and memories from my life. I saw my successes and mistakes. They all began to blur into whiteness.

When I decided it was time to leave the room, Mary asked me to turn off the lamp. I did. I turned around and walked out of the darkness into the bright light of the hall as if it were my guiding light. I felt joy in the memories but also sadness in that room. I felt so much loss of loved ones as though I were orphaned and alone. I turned around and closed the door.

The past may be overwhelmingly sad at times as we grieve what we have lost and in turn, creates our fear of loss in the future. Leaving the past and not dwelling on it is imperative. It doesn't mean we have to forget. We just have to turn out the light, close the door and step into the new bright light of what's ahead.

Everyone makes mistakes in life. Don't beat yourself up. Learn from the past so you don't make mistakes again. The fear level should go down with having gained some insight. The future does not have to be feared. After all, some day that future will also be the past.

So, I guess another secret of the heart is to let go of the sadness attached to memories and remember the good times. Look forward, not backward.

This session felt very surreal as though I was getting a life review. The old gray chair seemed like a catalyst that forced my mind to go back in time. I saw joyfulness and love as well as sadness with the loss of loved ones. There were so many emotions all at once that it was overwhelming. I felt I had to get out of there. Turning out the light was turning away from the past. The past will always be there, as it cannot be changed. All we can do is change ourselves to be better people and learn from the past. Mistakes in life are bound to happen. Learning from your mistakes is priceless. Taking a negative and turning it around to something positive is always a plus.

I guess the key to the "secrets of the heart" belongs to the heart and may open many doors of the mind and soul. I wonder how many doors there are and how many secrets are to be revealed.

Chapter 15

Guides and Teachers

Have you ever wondered if you have a spirit guide? Maybe you even asked that they make themselves known to you only to have nothing happen. In the past I certainly asked many times to no avail. It seems that spirit guides don't show up on demand, as we would like. Sometimes we are simply oblivious to their presence. We don't make connections easily as the density of the physical world dominates our senses. I believe guides are much wiser than us. They know when the time is appropriate to make themselves known though we may not recognize when it is happening.

      Many people believe there are no such things as guides or angels. Apparently, that does not deter guides or angels from doing their job. They seem to work in subtle ways. People are very quick to give a logical explanation for something that occurs for no reason as, "It is just a coincidence." How many times have you heard or said that very sentence? The word, coincidence, in my opinion, is too overused. Everything has a purpose no matter how insignificant. Even though it does not affect us directly, it could have an overall effect. After all, in a race, doesn't a fraction of a second make a difference in winning first place? EVERYTHING AND EVERYONE MATTERS.

The sessions in this chapter demonstrate the work of my guides, the first I refer to as the man with the vest.

Hall of Music
February 16, 2002

Some time ago, Zach, my son-in-law, was listening to me talk about the Gallery. It must have intrigued him enough to ask me if I thought I could find a place for music. It was both his curiosity as well as mine. With Mary's permission, I was shown what I call the Hall of Music. It was there that the man with the vest greeted me. Strangely, he seemed to have insight and understanding about Zach and me.

I visited Mary and, again, I was at the front door of My Place. She let me in. I wondered why she had me wait at the door. She laughed and said it is a joke. I don't get it.

Zach wondered if I could find the Hall of Music the way I did the Gallery. I asked her if I could and she said, "Yes." The next thing I knew, I was standing in front of a door and I had to press a doorbell. A gentleman answered the door. He had gray hair, kind of a mess, and a big gray mustache. He wore a vest under his suit. I stepped into a huge dome shaped empty room. On the left were windows that formed the shape of the room. I was aware of a theater nearby. The room was silent. I asked why the silence and he said, "Your art is visual, not auditory." I was told, "Zach is part of music. He is music. All he needs to do is listen and he will hear the unwritten music." I asked to see sheets of music. He said, "When you are prepared." I thanked the man for allowing me to see the Hall of Music.

Then suddenly, I was with Mary again in the Library. I thanked her too. She said, "Zach has to learn to listen to what is inside himself and eventually hear the music." I have to learn more about seeing.

Standing in this great Hall of Music I felt like I did not belong there. In a way it was eerie. I compared it to the way I imagine I would feel if I were alone in a large cathedral, empty, yet feeling an energy presence around me.

This session reinforced what I have known all along that Zach has so much musical ability that even he is not fully aware of the extent. Obviously, the man with the vest seemed to have knowledge of Zach's abilities and potential. It was made clear to me that my gift is the visual arts.

The Art Studio
May 10, 2009

Mother's Day. I wanted to say "Happy Mother's Day" to Mom and Mary. Searching for Mary in my mind, I found her in a beautiful garden in a park. I even saw blue birds that I thought were extinct and she said, "They are coming back." I asked to see my Mom and she showed me in the distance both Mom and Dad sitting on a bench. They looked young and were holding hands. I walked to see them and gave them a hug. It was strange because I looked older than my mother. I wished her Happy Mother's Day. In the distance, I saw her mother and her father's mother wave to us.

Then Mary said she had someone she wanted me to meet. We walked a little way and I saw a small building. We went in and there was an older gentleman, kind of short, a mustache and hair that was short and flared up over his ears. He wore a vest. The building looked like an art studio. Apparently, it was his. I asked who he was and he said it really did not matter, "It is the art that counts." I told him I need the inspiration to paint again and he showed me a door off his studio. He said it belonged to me at one time. I asked if I could see any of my paintings from my past life and he sadly said that they were destroyed in a fire in World War II. I asked if he knew who I was. He said I was one of the best but refused to tell me more. He did say I came from a small province in France.

The reason I have not painted much in this life is that I think on a deep level, "Why bother, the work must not have been good enough to save from the fire." The loss was so great, maybe it is not worth trying again. Is this my excuse? Perhaps depression from a past life has thwarted my efforts in this life. Now is my time to get over it. Not everything will be good but some will be excellent. He told me to return to the studio anytime I need inspiration. Clarity will come with frequency. Just draw.

It was good to see my parents in the park that day. They looked younger than I! It was a nice surprise. The man with the vest seemed to know me very well. By way of this session, it appears that in some past life I was an artist and I must have known this man. He indicated that we were neighbors. He also made a very important point. Perhaps it really does not matter who the artist is as he said, "It is the art that counts."

If the story is true, then maybe that energy of my soul was so severely depleted that it will take other life times to regain its strength. There are times in my present life where I feel like I am climbing up a sheer cliff trying to grasp inspiration to paint again. I can't look down for fear of falling. I keep telling myself, "I know I can do it." I just have to try. No, I have to do it!

In the following session, the man with the vest appeared in a different capacity.

Assessors' Office
January 24, 2011

I searched for Mary and could not find her. Instead, I stood to face a door. I focused on the door to make it clearer and I realized the door was old-fashioned as from an old office building. There was a heavy, frosted glass window above the door that was made of dark wood horizontal panels. The word, "Assessors" was written below the window. I opened the door and entered a room that looked like our old city hall offices with green painted walls, square floor tiles, and several desks. There were many people busy working. I noticed one desk in the back of the room that was empty and a comfortable looking chair next to it. Nobody noticed me as I sat in the chair behind the desk and asked, "Can anybody help me?" Then everyone stopped whatever they were doing, looked at me, and then immediately returned to their work.

A man came out from behind some files. He had a big

mustache, a three-piece suit and beautiful piercing blue eyes like I had never seen before. Then I noticed Mary sitting in another chair next to the desk but she did not say a word. The man placed a piece of paper on the desk and asked if I would sign it. I asked what it was. He said if I signed the paper, I would be removing all karmic debt. However, it was also my promise to use all my gifts. He said I have been given permission to write. So, I guess I signed my own contract to write a book. I'm working on it.

This was not the usual encounter with Mary. I could not imagine what I was doing in the Assessor's office. It was a new experience as the man with the vest showed up with a contract. I thought to myself, "What is he talking about with regards to karmic debt?" I certainly was not about to question it too much. It sort of sounded like a "get out of jail" card in monopoly. I remember signing the contract and seeing my hand write my name as clearly as I would in a fully conscious state.

I plan on using whatever "gifts" I have. I would be a fool not to use them. Everyone should use his or her gifts to the fullest. Why else would they have been given?

The Train
January 16, 2014

While thinking about the book, I decided to visit Mary again. Instead of the usual places, I was quite surprised to find myself sitting in a train. Mary was seated next to me. It felt like the train was moving fast. Looking out the window in front of me was a very pretty scene of tall green pines at the edge of a large blue lake.

Then the train practically stopped on a bridge over the water. I was alone with Mary until the conductor showed up. He wore a conductor's hat and a three-piece suit. I believe he is the same man I have seen a few times during my sessions. He quietly sat next to Mary.

Mary said that the train represented my life journey. I feel I am the only passenger on this train and not in control of where the train, or my life, is going. Even though this train seemed at first to be going fast, it was now almost stationary. It seemed to be struggling not to get stuck.

I think this means that I felt my life was moving too fast and I was not really noticing everything. It was a bit of a blur like looking out the window of a fast-moving train. Now it feels like I am slowly moving over this bridge.

I think I am finally beginning to see things clearer. I am noticing the details in the scenery, taking the time to slow down and allow myself the clarity of thought. The writing process has forced me to slow down and think. It has been difficult to sort out the book but I now have a plan. It will come about one chug at a time.

I asked Mary where I was headed and she just said it didn't matter. It's the journey that counts.

As I get older, I try to remember different times in my life. Some are definitely clearer than others. Sometimes I need a reminder either from old photos or old friends telling of pleasant times we had together. They will say, "Do you remember the time when..." and I respond, "Sure." when, actually I am having a hard time remembering. I feel a little guilty for the false acknowledgment and a little sad that I cannot share the same memory as my friend. The point is, life keeps moving faster but the retrieval of memories slows down as we age. Perhaps, as wisdom would dictate, if I had just paid more attention to "being in the moment," and took the time to cherish the emotions attached to an event, I would have more memories. Thank goodness my friends were paying attention!

The bridge that the train was chugging along is symbolic for the process of my slowing down and taking the time to enjoy life in my retirement years. It also seems to represent both a connection and separation something like ending a chapter and beginning a new chapter in a book.

I think the conductor, the man with the vest, came along for the ride. I felt this man was playing an important part in my life journey but, I still was not sure who he really was. I began to make the connection with the previous sessions. Could this be the same man?

The Reveal
December 2, 2014

When I visited Mary today, I found her in the garden. She looked radiant as usual. However, I told her I would feel more comfortable in the Classroom. Instantly, we were in the Classroom seated on the pew facing the window. She then got up, looked out the window and turned to me saying there was someone on the patio that I was to meet. Quite often that is where I have met someone who has passed. I could not imagine who would be there.

As I walked from the Classroom to the patio, I began to focus on details as I entered the Library. I noticed the wallpaper near the French door. It had a beige background that seemed to have a red, raised, velvety texture to the intricate pattern. The French door was a dark mahogany wood. I stepped onto the two gray granite steps that led to the patio. The outside borders of the patio were solid granite whereas the center was brick. The lawn was a beautiful green with a large, old, gnarled shade tree in the middle.

When I turned around to face the house, I noticed a man standing near the French doors. I recognized him as the gentleman whom I have seen before in previous sessions. The man was rather short in stature. He wore a gray three-piece suit. His messy hair reminded me of a famous picture of Albert Einstein. He wore a heavy mustache and had beautiful blue eyes. This was the same man who answered the door in the Hall of Music. During a past life regression, he showed me the art studio in France. He gave me the contracts to sign and he was the conductor on the train. This time, however, was very different.

He introduced himself to me shaking my hand and he said his name was Joseph. He stated, "I am the keeper of the gifts." He said he was my guide and teacher. Apparently, it was time for him to step in and help me. He took me into the Library and pointed to the books. He told me that I needed to use all the information in the books. I told him that I did not think I had enough time in my life to be able to do so and he retorted that my sense of time is not the same as time in My Place. Joseph spoke very authoritatively and curtly. I asked him if My Place is in the Astral Plane and he said, "No. It is much higher." I then asked, "If I don't use all my gifts, will I lose them?" His answer was, "Not necessarily."

I then stated that I have low self-esteem and not that

much confidence in myself. I did not think I could do all that he thought I should accomplish. He told me that those burdens were given to me, as I have to learn to conquer them in this life. No excuses. I have the intellect and talent to overcome these obstacles. It is my free will if I chose to do so. I felt it was time for me to leave.

As I opened my eyes I realized that I could hardly sense my extremities. I could see them yet felt disconnected from my hands and legs. I knew I could move them if I wanted to, but, in a way, it felt good to be so relaxed.

A dear friend of mine, Karen, who is able to see spirits, for years has been telling me that she could see a man with Joseph's description standing near me. She would ask me if I knew anyone who looked like that and I would always say, "No one I know, past or present." I never put two and two together until I read my journals for the umpteenth time. Oh boy, was I shocked when I made that connection. I could not believe it took me so many years to figure this out.

As far as the burdens that Joseph spoke of, being my concerns of low self-esteem and lack of confidence, I believe that I have been working hard to overcome the emotions attached to these burdens. He was right. There are no excuses for not trying to overcome obstacles in the way. When you are given the proper tools, you have an obligation to yourself to make the effort to improve. To accept our state of being as something that cannot be changed for the better is laziness in my opinion. I had become lazy and made too many excuses for myself. I had become complacent to simply accept that I had low self-esteem and no confidence in myself. Negative thinking sure is a downer.

There are so many inspirational stories of people who have accomplished amazing things despite their limitations. They chose to not accept defeat and instead saw it as an opportunity to discover strength from within. They made the choice and, now, so have I.

Finally, I am beginning to get answers to some of my questions. It makes sense that Joseph is the "keeper of the gifts." He was present in the Hall of Music, the art studio, the signing of the writing contract and the train checking on the progress of my book.

I also asked if My Place is in the "Astral Plane." Allow me to explain. Ancient theologians have depicted the Astral Plane as a realm in which our souls enter upon our death where we then spend a period of time before we move up to higher dimensions. You could say it is a space between heaven and earth. Apparently, My Place is a little higher up on the ladder according to Joseph.

Mary

For all the years I have visited Mary, I was not sure who she really was. At one point I had asked her if she was Mother Mary and she basically said if I thought that was who she was then so be it. No more explanation was needed at the time. The following session answered some questions.

Will the Real Mary Please Stand Up?
May 14, 2015

I decided to visit Mary today with nothing on my agenda. I found her in the garden in the usual place sitting on a bench under an arbor. I noticed some beautiful white flowers on a vine that had grown over the top of the arbor. I had never seen them before and I'm not sure what kind they were.

Mary then said she had something important to show me. Instantly I was standing on Memory Lane. She gently tapped my forehead and I could feel myself slipping into a deeper level of relaxation.

Suddenly, I witnessed a horrifying scene. There appeared to be cages built out of wooden branches that formed a dome-shaped structure similar to a birdcage. I was very much aware of smoke and fire as well as human screams and smelling burning flesh that sent a chill up my spine. I sensed I was a very young girl dressed in what appeared to be a burlap sack type of garment. I could feel sheer terror run through me to the point of being unable to move. Suddenly, I felt a strong jerk to my right arm as I was forcefully being pulled away from the commotion. I looked to see another girl appearing older than myself dressed in the same material. She was pulling me to safety.

A short amount of time passed and I could see us running in the woods eating berries on the way. Somehow, we came upon a dwelling and cautiously stole some clothing. We then managed to find a small town. Begging for someone to take us in, the older girl explained to the townspeople that we were orphaned and had no family. There we found refuge and peace.

The next moment, I was back in the garden confused and still shaken after what I had just experienced. Mary was by my side and proceeded to explain.

She said in that past life she was the older girl and I was the young one. She was my sister. According to Mary, she has been my sister throughout my many lifetimes. Sometimes I was the older sister. Mary stated that in my present lifetime, she chose to remain in spirit as she would be of more benefit to my spiritual evolution and help me progress. She said that she would always be there for me. There is a special bond that some sisters have as I have with my present earth sister. For me, it cannot be broken.

I see Mary as a beautiful woman with great wisdom. It seems she was always my protector throughout our many lives together. She had guided me and mentored me as only a good sister would. I feel her strength and understanding.

In this lifetime, she has taken on the role of spirit guide and teacher. She waited, as did Joseph, to reveal to me the role they have played in my life. I feel I have been blessed with their special gifts and they are much appreciated.

Chapter 16

The Turning Point

What happened?
July 10, 2016

    I decided to take some time for myself today and visit with Mary. I had nothing particular on my mind. I found myself standing in the Library facing the books when I realized that it was extremely bright in the room like sunlight everywhere. I looked up to see there no longer was a ceiling! I was looking straight up into the clear blue sky. Then suddenly, the walls of books started to disappear. I felt a strange sense of panic roll through me from my feet straight through to my hands. A book lay in my hands and as if by the wind that comes from a summer storm, each page was blown away until there were no more.
    Now a stronger sense of panic rushed through me as I ran to enter the Classroom. A moment of relief came over me as I thought that room was still intact only to be suddenly

aware of sunshine filling the Classroom. Again, the walls and windows began to disappear.

Instantly, I was standing in the meadow that once was viewed through the massive window of the Classroom. I then sensed the peacefulness that I had only imagined existed.

Suddenly, Mary was now with me in the field of grass and wild flowers. To say the least, I was stunned and a little frightened at what just occurred. She assured me that all was well. She explained that I no longer needed the mansion or the books. She said, "From this point on, experience will be your teacher."

All that I had come to know in this amazing mansion was gone in a few moments. So many questions left to be answered. How was I going to continue with this journey? What does all this mean? An odd sense of excitement intertwined with a feeling of great loss.

At first, I felt as though I had just graduated from school and I was being sent out into the real world. Now I realize the mansion was the schoolhouse providing all the necessary tools. The books and their symbolism taught me to look deeper into the meaning of living in this world. It helped open my mind to understand myself and know who I am.

The rooms I visited were comfortable and sheltering. Even the glass window in the Classroom, which separated me from the outside, was a protective barrier allowing me to see Nature as my teacher. Now I have the freedom to explore beyond the walls of books and mortar. I still have Memory Lane, The Secret Garden and everything else outdoors.

Now when I meet Mary, I find her standing near a huge tree. The tree is the same big, old elm tree that stood in front of our house when I was growing up. Mary has told me that the tree is symbolic of safety and of my strength. The branches allow me to continue to explore and make choices. Since this experience, I have asked Mary if the beautiful mansion will return and she simply says, "You don't need it anymore." It is but a memory now.

I guess you could think, "This must be the end of the journey." Somehow, I doubt that. It feels like another beginning. Maybe another adventure awaits me. Only time will tell.

The End

Epilogue

I believe we are all on a journey of self-discovery. It begins the day we are born and ends when we die. We are all put on this planet to learn lessons. It seems to me that our lives are tiny puzzle pieces carefully designed into intricate patterns put together at just the right moment by a higher power.

The journey my soul is taking is an adventure in learning who I am, and, in the process, I'm hoping that the lessons and insights in this book will help you along your journey. I believe we are all here to help each other grow spiritually, making the connection between this physical lifetime and the timelessness of our souls.

My mansion was unique to say the least. It is hard to say what was my favorite part. Certainly, the Library books were intriguing, a fascinating aspect of my journey. It is hard to comprehend their vast knowledge and wisdom. I was able to explore only a small portion of their richness. However, the books I did see were meant for me to study in this lifetime. Many of their lessons cannot be easily expressed in words. Sometimes, as demonstrated in the Book of Truth, feelings and just "knowing" are enough. If you recall, the round hole in the middle of the Book of Truth was symbolic, and words were not needed to express a knowing.

What have I gained from my experiences? In general, I have a greater appreciation for life. I don't take things for granted as all can disappear in a moment. Life is about change and growth as a person. It is about the energy of love and its power. I have learned to trust in myself, and, yet, be grateful knowing I am guided. My experiences have solidified my belief in a Higher Power with unconditional love for all of us.

I have now realized most of my shortcomings and strengths. I have faced my fears and accepted the challenge to overcome these obstacles. The fact that I am brave enough to publicly write about them in this book is a big step in the right direction.

It is not easy to take a good hard look at yourself. I'm not talking about the image you see in the mirror every morning but the person deep inside. What do *you* see? I have learned to look deeper and now I know who I am.

Throughout the course of writing the book, I was struggling to find inspiration to paint again. Finally, I realized that I had never really lost it in the first place. It was always there. I just needed to remember.

This book became a 20-year endeavor. All good things come to be in their own time. I sincerely believe that Spirit has guided me through the process.

Since the conclusion of my book, I have returned many times to My Place. The following, of late, is of significance in my journey.

The Future
May 10, 2019

Today, Mary showed me a partially opened door. I peeked inside only to see darkness. She told me to step into the room. I wasn't sure what I was stepping into but I trusted her.

As I placed my foot inside the room, the room lit up. I could clearly see that it was a modern-day gallery, quite unlike the gallery in My Place. She said the locked door with many keys is now open to me. As I turned to look at the door, it disappeared.

I believe she was showing me that the future shows great promise for my art as I have now begun to paint again. Mary has also reassured me that the mansion will return in my next life to, once again, allow me the opportunity to gather the great wisdom and knowledge within its walls as I continue my spiritual evolution.

I am convinced hypnosis helped to open the door to communication with Spirit. Spirit helped to open the doors to my inner self, helped me to accept and understand my soul wisdom. Spirit showed me that we are not alone on this journey and Spirit is always there to help. All we have to do is ask and have patience to wait for the answer.

About the Author

Janet Barako is a massage therapist, hypnotherapist and Reiki Master who has been in private practice for over 20 years. She taught hypnotherapy for ten years at a local community college along with her husband, Joseph.

The author graduated from Westfield State University with a degree in Fine Art and has won many awards for her work. She entered massage school shortly after graduation and also maintained a medical transcription business for 30 years.

Janet coauthored a cookbook entitled, "Yeast-Free, Wheat-Free, Sugar Sensitive Cooking and Feeling Good About It." This cookbook was one of the first of its kind to help people with a condition called, Systemic Candidiasis.

She resides in Massachusetts with her husband, Joseph, and near their family.

She can be contacted at: janetbarako@gmail.com

Made in the USA
Middletown, DE
21 July 2019